Eco*lo*nomy

Doing business and manufacturing differently

Emmanuel Druon

Published by:
Triarchy Press
Axminster, England

info@triarchypress.net
www.triarchypress.net

Copyright © Emmanuel Druon, 2015

The right of Emmanuel Druon to be identified as the author of this work has been asserted by him in accordance with the Copyright, Designs and Patents Act, 1988.

No part of this publication may be reproduced, stored in a retrieval system or transmitted in any form or by any means including photocopying, electronic, mechanical, recording or otherwise, without the prior written permission of the publisher.

All rights reserved.

[First published in French in 2012 by Pearson as *Écolonomies: Entreprendre et produire autrement.*

This substantially revised and updated edition has been translated by Kevin Balston.]

A catalogue record for this book is available from the British Library.

ISBN: 978-1-909470-86-6

Further resources can be found at:

www.triarchypress.net/ecolonomy

All royalties on sales of this book will be donated in full to the French state-approved non-profit organisation Pocheco Canopée Reforestation, for the reforestation of the Nord-Pas de Calais region.

'Whatever happens, the flame of Resistance will never go out'.
Charles de Gaulle, 18th June 1940

Contents

Preface by Rob Hopkins 9

PART ONE ~ Doing Business and Manufacturing Differently 13

Chapter 1 ~ Idealistic, pragmatic and militant: our manifesto 15

Chapter 2 ~ A dominant model on its last legs 19

Chapter 3 ~ SMEs: the perfect testing ground 29

Chapter 4 ~ Acting for sustainable development 41

PART TWO ~ Practising What We Preach 49

Chapter 5 ~ Raw materials: leaving nothing to chance 51

Chapter 6 ~ Ecolonomy and life cycle assessment (not as bad as it sounds) 57

Chapter 7 ~ Managing energy, from the basement to the attic 65

Chapter 8 ~ Our waste is a treasure! 77

PART THREE ~ Finding Pleasure in Working as a Team 83

Chapter 9 ~ Giving the company a future 85

Chapter 10 ~ Ecolonomy Valley begins with us 89

Chapter 11 ~ The company, a pool of talent and activities 97

Chapter 12 ~ Multiplying initiatives, even not for profit ones 107

PART FOUR ~ A New Company Model 113

Case Study: Guy Watson, founder of Riverford Organic Farms 115

Interview: Éric Sauvage, Co-founder and manager of TexEurop 121

Conclusion 129

Notice 133

Acknowledgements 135

To dear Yazid Bousselaoui, for his worldly curiosity, his heartfelt intelligence and the integrity of his standpoints.

To the team:

Abdelaziz, Ahmed, Alain, Aline, Amar, André, Annie, Avishane, Bouchra, Bruno, Carine, Catherine G, Catherine L, Cédric, Christelle, Christian A, Christian D, Christian F, Christian L, Christophe, Cindy, Daniel, David G, David P, David S, Denis, Dorothée, Elizabeth, Elodie, Emmanuel, Eric, Fezzia, Fissa, Fouad, Franck B, Franck D, Fred Erick, Frédéric, Gaétan, Gerald, Guillaume Dec., Guillaume Def., Guy, Halef, Hayat, Jacky, Jean Michel, Jean Paul, Jean-Marc, Jennifer, Joël, Johan, Jonathan F, Jonathan H, Julien, Kaddour, Kevin, Lamir, Laurence, Laurent Bar., Laurent Bau., Laurent F, Laurent H, Loïc, Ludovic, Malik, Marie Christine, Marlène, Maryline, Maryse G, Maryse R, Maurice, Maxime, Mehdi D, Mehdi Z, Melody, Mickaël B, Mickaël D, Miguel, Moaz, Mohammed Saïd, Muriel, Mustapha, Nadia, Nadine, Nasser, Nathalie A, Nathalie M, Nick, Nicole, Pascal H, Pascal S, Patrick, Philip, Philippe, Raphaël, Raynald, Saïd, Sébastien M, Sébastien P, Sébastien T, Sonia, Sophie, Stéphanie, Théo, Thierry, Valérie, Van Phi, Xavier, Yasmina, Yves

…with whom everything seems possible and probable, for whom it is all worthwhile and without whom nothing (or almost) would make any sense.

To my parents (the poor things!).

But also to all the trees we are going to plant. To our future children. To the irreplaceable Réjean. And to doubt.

Preface

As I sit down to write this, the British Prime Minister, David Cameron, has just announced that the UK government is going "all out for shale gas". Faced with crippling rates of decline for oil and gas production in the North Sea, the UK has decided that the shale gas revolution taking place across the Atlantic in the USA can be replicated in the UK. Communities are to be bribed with money for each well drilled, and local authorities will be allowed to keep all the business rates – very attractive as the austerity drive cuts their funding hard.

The climate scientists tell us that the best, indeed the only, place for shale gas is to remain hundreds of feet below the ground. Yet we remain fixated on the idea that our only way forward is to keep doing what we've always done in the way we've always done it, even if that leads us to an uninhabitable planet. But there is another way, and that other way is the subject of the book you have just started reading.

For the last seven years, I have been part of a worldwide experiment to explore what a bottom-up response to the challenges of the 'New Normal' we currently live in might look like in practice. Motivated by concerns about climate change, the end of the age of cheap energy, and the fragile and volatile economy on which we depend, it has proposed doing things rather differently. We call it the Transition movement, and it is now active in 44 countries around the world, building more resilient communities from the bottom up. Alongside the need to reduce carbon emissions it sees the need to strengthen local economies in order to build in resilience to times of rapid change.

In recent years, it has moved from being a community-organising strategy to very deliberately being about starting new economies from the ground up. It argues that rather than imagining a future where the last of the world's fossil fuels are squeezed out in order to sustain economic growth at all costs, there is a different economy we could create. One that is much more local, meeting as many of its needs locally as possible – what we call 'appropriate localisation'. One that is framed around building resilience, the ability to withstand and learn from shocks. One that respects the idea of living within natural limits and which is inherently low carbon in all that it does. It will also, where possible, bring assets into community ownership, and be about more than just generating profit, having a social return to what it does.

Through Transition Network's REconomy Project, we are supporting many initiatives around the world that are putting this into practice. In some places, we have done detailed local economic analyses, building the economic case for a more localised economy. We start to see what the economy of the future will look like, taste like and, sound like. We're seeing amazing community energy companies, local currencies, innovative new local food models, community farms, new craft breweries, community-supported bakeries and much more.

In doing this work, we are always scanning the horizon for inspiration, for models of enterprises that have already successfully done this. This is not a time for reinventing the wheel. One of those that has appeared, a shining beacon on the horizon, is Pocheco, the envelope factory with the beehives on the roof. A business that puts its minimisation of water, waste and energy use at the heart of what it does. That thinks through its use of materials and strives to walk as lightly on the earth as possible. But that's a story you will be told in the pages to come.

It's a story that matters because it shows that, at the fork in the road at which we stand, it is not only possible to turn away from the fracking wells, the tar sands fields, the 6°C climate change the International Energy Agency say will be the result of 'business as usual'… it could be the making of us. As we stand at that fork, where is the creativity, the inventiveness, the passion? It took phenomenal imagination to create an industrial revolution in the first place, it will take something similar to create what happens next. That's what I love so much about the story you are about to hear. It doesn't present the process of stepping forward responsibly into the future as being a dour process of doing without and slowly returning to live in caves. It is about a visionary, Emmanuel Druon, setting out to reimagine Pocheco from the ground up, reducing its environmental impact, preventing pollution, reducing risks at work and lowering the burden of work, and making a financial profit by improving the productivity of the plant and the organisation.

While the many technologies and approaches which are set out in these pages are fascinating and replicable, what I hope you take away with you is a spirit, a sense that anything is possible. The scale of transformation, of transition, that the world must undertake over the next 10 to 20 years is historically unprecedented. If we manage it, our children and grandchildren will sing great songs and tell great tales of what we did in these times. One of those stories will be about Pocheco. Will one of them also be about what you did once you finished this book?

Rob Hopkins is the co-founder of Transition Town Totnes and Transition Network. He is author of *The Transition Handbook*, *The Transition Companion* and *The Power of Just Doing Stuff*. In 2010 he was awarded a PhD by the University of Plymouth, and in 2013 an Honorary Doctorate by the University of the West of England. He blogs and tweets regularly, recently co-founded a social enterprise craft brewery and is a keen gardener.

www.transitionnetwork.org

PART ONE

Doing Business and Manufacturing Differently

Let's start with a shocking revelation: I am not what you would call over-qualified. I just scraped through my university literature degree at Sorbonne VI in Paris in the 1980s. But I'm not going to bore you with the usual life story of the self-taught and (almost) complacent businessman, who doesn't want to question his habits, and certainly doesn't want to change them, along the lines of, "I did it my way, no one helped *me*, I started from nothing…" Because who cares? Many companies began with a personal adventure that turned out well and which, through intelligence and hard work, found its niche. Does that mean we can do any old thing we please? No, it does not.

Nevertheless, I have an opinion. I think that if the dominant economic model were working well, we would certainly know about it! There would be less hardship and fewer people falling by the wayside at home and abroad. What I suggest is that we think things through differently. We can do this by questioning both what is apparently obvious and a number of truths that are, we're repeatedly assured, carved in stone.

Multinational giants may very well carry on playing dinosaurs for a few more years, exhausting non-renewable resources through their arrogance and blindness. We, the people, will probably be able to do nothing about it… for a while. But, if the (more or less silent) hordes of small companies and their teams, like us, count for nothing on their own, together we *can* move things forward and give weight to our actions. We can plan balanced development for our businesses without basing everything we do on growth. Besides, nothing grows forever.

So then, how can we 'eco*lo*nomise'? I suggest we think about a few simple and efficient rules. We've been using them in our company for over fifteen years and we're still here to tell the tale!

Chapter 1

Idealistic, pragmatic and militant: our manifesto

People often pitch ecology against realism in the Western world, where the market economy is accorded almost cult status. So is it realistic to be an ecologist, from the viewpoint of business?

As far as I'm concerned, this debate is old hat. But I understand why so many businesspeople hold such opinions. For them, economic concerns take precedence over everything else, often justifiably: customers want good prices. Meaning lower, ever-lower prices. This concern is pivotal, because no one can afford to lose a customer. Moreover, the question of *growth* is always central. And we rarely question it.

Querying our relationship to the economy, or our relationship to growth, boils down to asking whether or not the dominant model of the market economy can be called into question. I think it has to be. Does that make me a revolutionary?

I am one of the generation born in the twenty years after the end of World War Two. We have seen nothing but economic crises ever since we entered the job market. And so I can legitimately express doubts and ask a few questions about the validity of the current system.

The apocalyptic way in which our environmental situation is presented is a source of general despondency which, according to our individual sensitivities, sometimes throws us into a state of cold panic. As citizens of the rich West we feel responsible and guilty, at least sometimes. The issue is far too serious and there is no time for disinformation, 'lobbying', intellectual laziness or lack of integrity. As citizens, employees or unemployed, businesspeople, civil servants, craftspeople or farmers, we must make it our business to be well-informed about economics, society, the environment and our ecology.

And that is one of the goals I've set myself with this book: to dismantle certain preconceived ideas. We cannot allow ourselves to be satisfied with distorted and biased information, itself in turn often bolstered by ignorance and disinformation (whether intentional or not).

Ideally (by which I mean on the level of our ideals), we cannot accept this situation. We dream of something different, not only for future generations but also for ourselves. We sometimes find ourselves irrationally longing to stop the glaciers melting, right now, as if by magic! Faced with the seriousness of the situation, we have the confused feeling that some magic force might be able to reverse what is happening. This is a kind of omnipotence that, rationally, we know is out of our reach.

We also feel that the time for simple wishful thinking is past. The all-too-common 'All we need to do is...' is not a solution. In the end, who can we turn to sort out our problems? Politicians? Our neighbours?

So then, what can we do to act constructively? Best case scenario: we give a donation to a charity working in the areas that concern us. Then we do nothing else – no follow-through. And still one more catastrophe follows another, relentlessly. A feeling of fatigue overtakes us, leading to despair.

We need to take individual responsibility with every single one of our actions. All the time. I can see no other way of acting on a personal level. We may not have the tools for large-scale action but we do possess our own free will. And, every day, every gesture counts. I hope you'll give it a try once you've finished this book.

At Pocheco, a small company in the north of France, we have decided to take action. At our own level, as best we can. We have committed ourselves to acting consistently, both in the company in every project we're involved in, and also outside of work. Companies are not places for militancy but, for those people fortunate enough to be in work, they *are* a place to think about each gesture we make. And altering our gestures, day by day, in line with the best information we can lay our hands on, soon has an impact. Here, we consider ourselves citizens *in* the workplace as well as outside it.

At Pocheco, each investment has to meet the three indispensable criteria we have set for ourselves. Investments must bring about:

- a measurable reduction in our impact on the environment
- a measurable reduction in how difficult or dangerous individual jobs are
- measurable increases in productivity.

This means that each investment gives rise to one or more 'eco*lo*nomies'.

The idea that green manufacturing or building costs an average of 20% more than so-called traditional methods is well-established in most people's minds. But here we demonstrate that this notion has had its day. It is (in fact) cheaper to manufacture cleanly!

This book demonstrates the validity of the concept of 'eco*lo*nomy' as implemented in small or medium-sized companies. And I will also refer to a range of books and documents which can provide further reading on the subject.

Everything explained here concerns our own production site. So, can eco*lo*nomy be put into practice in *your* company or in *your* home? Allowing for differences in scale, the answer is yes. In fact, we often take inspiration from what a member of our team has tried out at home and adapt it to our production site.

Although I practise what I preach, I still have many bad habits which I need to review and change. But if, day by day, more and more of us quietly alter the way we act, to reflect the kind of information and knowledge set out here, then maybe it's not too late for us all to begin living better: more responsibly, more accountably, more wisely. In any case, there's no good reason *not* to change.

If, at the same time as delivering useful products to our customers, we could reduce the environmental impact of our industrial activity and contribute to slowing climate change, we might reach a point where our working lives would be less stressful and, surely, less guilt-ridden. We would feel happier about things.

So, fasten your seat belts! We are in for a bumpy ride! I shall be forthright. My aim is to show you how we have broken down the barriers that others have erected for us, or that we have sometimes erected ourselves, through lack of time, energy or information. I am defending a point of view and my use of language will sometimes betray a certain warrior spirit. I admit this because I happen to feel that we have joined the 'resistance'. The time for resistance has come.

Chapter 2

A dominant model on its last legs

The dominant model needs to be re-examined mainly in the area of financial independence. Companies must take their freedom back into their own hands. To do so, they need to question their rate of growth. This includes company size, the model of financial shareholders obsessed with getting a return on their investment and, finally, the ways in which companies are governed.

Is growth a question of size?

How many times have I heard this old line, "You won't survive if you stay medium-sized!" Medium-sized in relation to what? What are they on about? Critical mass and the race for growth... This is where the choice of economic and financial vocabulary gets interesting!

Growth is seen to be *the* solution. If things pick up, everything will get better. Better? Everything will go faster more like, straight into oblivion. There will be exhaustion of natural resources and of people, forced into impossible rates of output in the name of consumption. Consumption itself is seen as an overriding necessity – the legitimacy of which we never see fit to question. Don't fret, I'm no supporter of degrowth. I quite simply note that, in our line of business, we get by on 1% growth, or no growth at all, without having to shut up shop.

If your business operates in a niche or specialist area, then it can be an advantage being a medium-sized company, if only because the heads of such companies take personal responsibility for product quality and the results they promise. I don't believe it's possible to build a serious business on unkept promises. A lot of time and energy must first be put into understanding the customer's individual requirements, the context in which these requirements have arisen and the underlying reasons why they have shown an interest in your product/service or your company. Then you have to work hard with your team to create the conditions for success, meaning the customer's complete satisfaction.

Such is the situation in our company. Our customers are mostly 'key accounts'. Serving such customers means being constantly on the ball as regards their ever-changing needs and ways of working. We have to be thorough every step of the way. I often compare the organisation of our industrial work to that of a farmer ploughing a field, remaining humble because the work is hard and results take a long time; or to that of a craftsman who has, in part, automated the company to cope with increased demand, but who is under no obligation to become world number one.

Is financial shareholding the only model to follow?

What if company profitability were no longer an aim in itself, but were to become a means of doing business (once again)?

Of course, that would mean giving up on rapid growth and accepting a process which might take decades, even generations, to complete. It would mean investing in facilities (industrial ones, in our case), all the while staying on the course you set yourself in the first place. It would mean listening to the market and, more directly, the customers – the managing director should know each and every one of them. He or she should also meet them regularly, so as to understand their requirements inside out. That implies having *and taking* time.

For forty years, all the money made by Pocheco has been ploughed wholly and systematically back into the company, without exception. It has gone into research and development, renewing machinery, training, safety improvements, recycling and energy savings and, outside the company, into reforestation. This means that we can function perfectly independently: we do not pay out dividends and have no gluttonous shareholders demanding yearly returns of 15%. We are, therefore, firmly in the black as far as cash flow is concerned and our level of equity reassures both bankers and partners.

Our bank rating is E3+ (which confirms our good health).[1] All the same, our sector, like so many others, is going through rough times.

---

1. The E represents a business volume of between €15 and €30 million. 3+ shows the company's capacity to honour its financial commitments. This is the second-best grade out of a list of twelve.

Among other things, the implication for the head of this company is that there will be no brilliant career path. It means toiling away loyally. A beast of burden ploughing the field with slow but sure steps in the first chill of autumn with steam billowing from its nostrils!

That's what going into business means. Not: 'Quick! Let me cash in, accumulate, move on, move back, cheat, hire, use, fire, take advantage, and nothing for anyone else'. *That* is not doing business. *That* is something else entirely, trying to fill a bottomless pit. Operating in such a way doesn't allow you to work with the aim of lasting and growing, all the while taking employees, customers and investors into account and, at the same time, remaining attentive to environmental questions.

Luckily, not all bosses are vandals with the sole idea of making a fortune. Not all private companies are managed by demented 'relocators' who only care about short-term, private interests.

The fine balance of governance

Does growth depend on the way a company is governed? Should we stay at the head of the same company all our lives? As naïve as that may sound, many company directors would do well to ask themselves this very question. I consider that, at a certain point, the time will come to pass operational authority on to someone else. I talk about this with my team, because such decisions need time to mature and there are no magic answers. I know that change will inevitably come. It may even be that writing this book is an important step in the process.

All the same, Nicolas Hayek, the brilliant developer of Swatch who took over some of the great names of Swiss clock-making, said in an interview towards the end of his life that an entrepreneur is an artist. Who would think of asking a painter to lay down his brushes because he is over legal retirement age? It's certainly worth thinking about.

Handing over the reins is a crucial question. Any company which is born and grows, will one day die. I am not attempting the impossible by programming what will become of the company long after the current team has finished. But I *do* have to plan a hand-over that will keep our efforts alive over the next generation. Part of the answer lies in 'demonetisation'; in other words, company property must not be allowed to generate profits for a few to the detriment of the whole. We are studying the possibility of becoming a corporate foundation or a worker cooperative, two structures which cater for cooperative company management.

There must be clear rules for governance which give financial questions the right level of importance. Or, to put it another way, rules which allow the company, or its senior management structure, to generate the means for autonomous development, any profits from which go towards strengthening company equity and *not* towards lining the pockets of an heir to the fortune. Employees and management will be paid salaries for their hard work. From this point of view, the study of how non-governmental organisations (NGOs) and non-profit organisations have developed is extremely enriching.

I consume, therefore I am

Growth and consumption are inextricably linked. Growth in the respect we pay to the environment, and growth in our capacity to respond to, and meet, customers' real needs, has to be based on a new way of consuming.

Now, the continuity of the current model depends on the consumer being treated as a marketing target with predictable, stereotypical behaviour. This is what makes us unthinkingly swallow the fallacies we hear. It is also why we accept unbridled consumption as a fact of life and why we demand low prices under any conditions. And then we are surprised at the damage this system causes! Let's be coherent about it and begin by refusing to consume just for the sake of consuming!

Let's be a bit more public-spirited!

It can be done, if we only buy what we really need and ensure that it is of good quality. Everything is linked: if something is made locally (in our own country or economic area), the price takes into account the welfare system, state schools, upkeep of roads and support for the poorest among us. If something is made locally, then the price covers the taxes that we pay and social cover that we receive.

As heavily as we may criticise our welfare system for its management (but could *we* do any better in their shoes?), these systems protect us all. We should not (conveniently) forget this when choosing between a local product and a foreign one.

Local manufacturing in Europe is alive and kicking! There are many products you can buy less frequently than Asian imports, because they will last you for years.

It can be done, little by little, as long as we change our bad habits as consumers caught up in the extreme conditions of the neo-liberal system and globalisation. It can be done, step by step, one gesture at a time, starting now.

Importers, supplying tons of badly-made products, often manufactured in inhuman conditions such as you would not wish on anyone, with dubious raw materials, can change the way they work, if we help them.

Imagine deciding not to buy any more 'exotic' products. There would be less shipping around the world, fewer factory closures close to home and more jobs protected. It's something we can work on every day and concerns every one of us. Perhaps much more so than you think. You can buy all sorts of 'local' goods, ranging from a basket of seasonal fruit and vegetables grown in your area under integrated farm management, to a microwave oven built by a company near you, a book published and printed locally, honey or butter from your region… even a paper envelope made in the Nord-Pas de Calais!

Don't misunderstand me, I'm neither advocating self-sufficiency nor protectionism. But I am not convinced that our children absolutely *need* the last word in plastic toys to play with at school. I understand how difficult it is to say no to a child, after a stressful day when you're stuck in traffic on the way home. But it gets easier if we remember that resources are limited and that our everyday actions are playing a major part in their destruction.

The diktat of low prices, a vicious circle

Pocheco works very little with mass-market retailers. Our product is poorly suited to that sector. However, the purchasing methods used in these circles have spread their poison to all sectors and, most noticeably, into the minds of nearly all purchasers. They justify almost anything in the name of cutting costs. There can be verbal violence or threats. Relocations destroy jobs close to home (this situation can easily affect the families of the very purchasers who steamroll suppliers) and give them to less well-paid and less well-protected workers. These relocations dramatically increase the road-miles involved in the transport of raw materials and finished products.

'Anything goes' in the name of price. All this without even mentioning the pressure applied, the unkept promises, the lop-sided contracts, the draconian conditions imposed on many suppliers, which can rule out local companies and those too small to resist.

All because the sledgehammer argument in the market economy is that, in order to sell products, you have to win over new consumers and, therefore, achieve lower production costs. Once more, the centralised retail circuit of the supermarket chains has played a major rôle here. And with it has grown the idea that, if only short-term profit and low prices matter, then product quality and durability must, even if this has never been official, take a back seat – so that they have now become the least important factors of all. This is a vicious circle, where lower prices lead to lower production costs, then to a drop in quality. It has contributed to the rapid expansion of the intercontinental transport industry, with no thought for the people concerned – neither those who have lost their jobs, nor those living in the Dark Ages in other countries. No thought either for the unreasonable use of toxic substances. Not an eyebrow raised in surprise at the accelerated depletion of raw materials. Simply because the essential point is the price.

We need to turn the issue on its head.

It can be done if products are made with attention to quality, making sure that each element of the supply chain follows the same rules.

It can be done if we invest our revenue in research, equipment, maintenance and training, which is only possible if we stop giving in to the organised blackmail and racketeering of shareholders demanding 10 or 15% annual returns!

It can be done if we keep companies at a size where human contact remains possible.

It can be done if we reduce stress: stress due to working hours, stress from rigid or zero-hours contracts, stress from tense or non-existent staff relations (have you ever been in the lift with a manager who didn't return your 'hello'?), stress because of badly-maintained machinery...

This way, we will regain the room for manœuvre we need to ensure the sustainability of our businesses. We are the generation that has to rise to the occasion and act decisively. The whole way we behave and reason needs to change. "Is it a revolt?" "No, Sire. It's a revolution." And, quite frankly, it is very exciting, incredibly stimulating. This revolution is probably extremely profitable in the medium term, and it will bring with it many pleasant surprises. Best of all, the problems that come with it are not insurmountable,

Let's think 'glocal'!

I was chatting to a supermarket department supervisor a few months ago. I wanted to buy a microwave oven for the company canteen. I was looking for one made in France. I set the alarm off as I was turning the display models round to check where they were made. The salesperson approached me with a tense expression on his face. I told him what I was after and he started looking with me. In the end, we found one which seemed to be made in the European Union. He warned me that it was not the cheapest one. I asked him from what point of view. From that of jobs in Europe? From that of the (very basic) checks on materials used and working conditions in China? From that of the ecological cost of container transport? He said, "No, from the point of view of the sale price". But he bounced back by explaining that, indeed, maybe that was not the only factor we should be taking into consideration. There *is* a price difference, about 15%. Naturally, there are people for whom that counts. But have they ever thought about buying a machine which, instead of doing the job for two years, lasts twice as long?

It all depends on whether we buy a product or expertise ethically, or if we just look for a low price without worrying about what will happen later. So that consumers can buy ethically, it might at first be preferable to produce less but better, in other words well-designed and durable merchandise (a good example is Fiscars scissors from Finland).

Fighting relocation

Like you, I think unemployment is a catastrophe. Like you, I think our generation should contain it and begin to reduce it, until it disappears completely. Like you, I do not think employment is a goal in itself, but a means to an end. In any case, this is a subject that needs more emphasis placed on it in global economic thinking.

A first step would be less reliance on company relocations. That would certainly help. Let me explain... Many companies which were tempted by the allure of relocating, or outsourcing, abroad have since come home. They worked out the cost of setting up production in an emerging country against profits available through competitiveness in the industrialised world. Frankly, so much the better! This upsurge in relocations back home is not yet happening across the board, but at least big companies are considering better-balanced distribution of their activities (that is, where these activities are not related to accessing new geographical markets).

As regards my company, whenever I say that I see no use in relocating, more often than not I detect a hint of sympathy or disdain in the other person's eyes. They must imagine that I am going to lose everything. First, market share, then whole markets; it will all be over for me in under ten years.

But that hasn't happened yet. On the contrary.

The last time an economic model, the Soviet model, was seen as the only one possible, the only realistic one, things went badly wrong. The current single model, glorifying relocation and outsourcing and extolling shareholders above all others, seems as dangerously monolithic to me as the Soviet one. Why should we all follow the same path, like lemmings?

A question of individual responsibility

Of course, I don't have all the answers. More specifically, I am not familiar with all the ins and outs even of national-level finance and taxation; far from it. But I cannot just sit back and watch unemployment follow as companies relocate or close down. I believe that, as consumers, we must take personal responsibility for every choice we make and that we must at least think about these things before making a purchase. It is an important subject because, in the name of low prices, we are all taking part in an organisational and logistical aberration that is destroying jobs and non-sustainable resources.

Let's come back to the supermarket where I was buying a microwave. The salesman had been listening more attentively for a minute or two and admitted that his wife had been laid off that very morning. She had been working for an industrial subcontractor. The workshop was relocating to Romania and she had been offered a job there for a quarter of her salary.

For whose benefit? For what profit? In the end, how many people make anything out of this system? Just think, the same thing could happen to you... And yet we do nothing about it! We do nothing and yet our whole democratic system is designed to spread and balance power, not to deliver profit to a small minority. Believing that you too will one day dine with the 'elite' is as much use as hoping that you'll win the lottery.

If we as citizens, entrepreneurs, employees, the unemployed, pensioners or civil servants do not react, it's because we really have accepted this system. We live with, and will continue to live with, its consequences. Otherwise, we are the ones who must find something to replace it with. Especially as solutions do exist. Genuine, efficient and long-lasting solutions.

Pascal Canfin demonstrates[2] that the number of jobs lost through the far-reaching changes in our habits if we were to adopt a more ecologically and socially respectful way of living would be outweighed by the number of jobs created. Such a change would mean new professions and more services in the general public interest. The positive balance for the 27 member states of the European Union would be 10.3 million jobs. What are we waiting for?

I'm not saying that life will be completely rosy if we make such changes. But honestly, looking at the strained faces on the metro and in traffic jams, I do not feel our consumer society is bringing us much peace of mind. All this tension and harshness in the contact we have with one another, along with the fatalism we find all around us, cries out for us to take stock of what we want and what we do not want any longer as a society. Moreover, this is what your vote should be used for, expressing your deep-rooted values by finding, searching for or even setting up your own movement. We *can* live differently!

It will take work and effort, but it can be done without violence or any life-changing sacrifices. On the contrary.

---

2. *Le Contrat écologique pour l'Europe*, Pascal Canfin, Les Petits Matins, 2009, pp.138-141.

Chapter 3

SMEs: the perfect testing ground

These days, we talk of ourselves as consumers rather than citizens, which really raises my hackles! 'Citizen' is such a beautiful word! It's so full of meaning and has such a wealth of history. Are we in the process of forgetting that we are citizens, meaning individuals participating in our society and bestowed with rights and duties such as the right to vote, to discuss and to debate?

The official line hammered into us is that the crisis the West is facing will only come to an end when growth returns. Everything must be done to support growth, because that will bring back purchasing power and consumption. Our society is doped on consumption and growth, rather like a stomach with no brain or heart. How will we manage when natural resources start to run out?

We must become citizens once more! We must act!

Personal involvement on all levels

Personal involvement is an essential element in any company, and it must begin with management. When I took over as managing director at Pocheco in 1997, I decided to establish fair relations between people. I wanted to calm the situation down between the workers and the management team and bring improvements in terms of health and safety but also more widely. And we have continued to work on this ever since. Clearly, I didn't do it all by myself. Everyone decided to pitch in. For example, my team and I together looked into the way we make the inks we use. We made a collective decision to cut out all solvents and to choose water-based inks instead.

In another example, technicians and all employees spend 30% of their working time in training. This enables them to become more versatile and means that they perform better in and beyond their jobs.

Allowing employees to take responsibility and get involved really lets them show the best of themselves. They are also usually more than willing because they gain as much from it as the company does. It's obvious that a working method which allows people to think about and act on difficulties in their jobs, as well as the environmental impact, all the while increasing productivity, has every chance of improving their own comfort at work and their pay.

This kind of employee involvement, which was taken on board quite naturally by staff at Pocheco, has resulted in such increased efficiency that we have been able to do away with three levels in our hierarchy.

In a highly competitive context, such employee involvement makes all the difference. Visitors notice it when they come to Pocheco. They always appreciate the fact that people here, despite having difficult jobs, are smiling, welcoming, open to others and to the world outside.

Away from the company, on another level entirely, how can the citizen get involved? Take our behaviour when faced with the greenwashing tactics of some companies. We have to recover the citizen in us, in other words understand what we need and refuse what we don't need. We need to gather information from multiple sources in order to make sense of the messages that different media seem to be constantly throwing at us. We have to tread carefully, at the same time avoiding paranoia that they are plotting against us.

I believe in a critical mind developed by experience and learning. I have observed that a critical mind, somewhat like a muscle, tends to wither through lack of use. A critical mind feeds on reading, not necessarily the daily press but, rather, the classics – so we can slowly come round to those great minds who dedicated their lives to refining thought. We have to demand more of ourselves. The wonderful state school system opens the world up to us. When we work with children, we rediscover forgotten books and reactivate what we already know. In middle age, we should re-read books that we forgot on leaving school. We need to exercise our memory and regain our notion of what history and geography mean, in addition to public spirit, as well as learning how to live as part of society once more. Above all, we are citizens before being consumers.

Our critical mind can also be put to work when we are faced with the stupefying advertising campaigns brought to us by the media. If we look at them analytically, we can easily pick out the half-truths and omissions they are littered with and which are, in fact, big fat lies. These little victories help us to take back control. It is, quite frankly, a question of exercising our personal judgement and discrimination instead of just 'absorbing' indiscriminately.

Being citizens at work as well as outside, we will continue to question the realities on display in our professional lives too, as we view them with the benefit of our newly-rediscovered critical faculties. And here I stress my view that, as regards the direction the world will take, we can have more say in the changes we're facing than is normally believed to be the case.

I am not saying that the return to common sense will be easy and effortless – just that it's unavoidable and is our own individual and collective responsibility. We *can* reduce discomfort, stress and suffering in the workplace, we *can* reduce unemployment, we *can* reduce the impact of our activities on the environment, we *can* offer a less dark future to generations yet to come. We can and we must, out of respect to ourselves.

Encouraging empowerment

Company change must also work in human terms. Multiple hierarchical levels pose a real problem as regards efficiency in general and communication in particular, especially when there are no clear rules about each person's individual decision-making capacity.

It's often believed that rules and procedures put in place by managers will help get the message across. But I think this is a big mistake. You only need to see the accumulated frustrations of people working for major companies. They spend an incredible amount of time describing company policies and saying how fed up they feel, but also how powerless they are. They say that they never make any real decisions. When they do finally decide on something, their choices may be called into question or swept away in one meeting.

This is particularly clear when the subject of ecological choices comes up. Our consultancy business specialising in industrial ecol*o*nomy, POCHECO Canopée Conseil, suggests solutions which sometimes bring about minor changes, or at other times more far-reaching ones, but they are always achievable. The people we deal with in client companies often, in fact almost always, get involved. They want to take part, at their own level, in improving the climate situation. When they understand we are not dressing up highly polluting procedures as greenwashing, they join in willingly. They do it because they want to.

Then, all of a sudden, a thousand difficulties will appear. A dozen meetings will be needed to make the smallest of decisions and the process becomes so complicated that, very often, they give up on the whole idea.

This even happens at the French Ministry of the Environment. There, representatives of our profession can take several months discussing how a new law will be be applied (with the relevant decrees being published much later). Negotiations are fruitful. An agreement might even be reached... Until, during a meeting towards the end of the process, a higher-ranking, or more authoritarian, civil servant sweeps away the result of months of negotiations with a single sentence. And when they've spoken, everything has to start again from scratch.

That can be acceptable if everyone involved knows the rules of the game; but often they don't. Even when the rules are clear to all concerned they often change, during negotiations, in favour of one of the supposedly stronger, hence more dominant, parties. Clever people work the system. They protect themselves and hide behind the hierarchy. This opens the door to all kinds of distortion and manipulation and it becomes so hard to understand the way things work that numerous 'short cuts' present themselves, ranging from corruption to influence or corporatism. The whole system stagnates and ends up fossilised.

From that point on, everything stops, leaving no room for change, innovation or creativity which are, in my view, the best means that human intelligence possesses for dealing with and solving difficulties.

Messages are distorted by so many intermediaries. The answer is delegation, on condition that everyone agrees to certain principles and that each link in the chain is given total freedom of action. That is to say, freedom to think, decide and then act. In short, freedom to take responsibility and to shoulder the consequences of their own actions.

Micro action is still action!

Every thought, every gesture, every conversation counts, whether in the context of the family or the company. I see this every day at work.

Like you, I understand the increasing distress of whole populations threatened by scarcity of drinking water (we're talking of the suffering and death of millions of human beings around the world). Conversely, I see catastrophic floods leaving whole populations in total disarray. Public policy is often powerless in these cases, so what are we to do? Close the paper, take a beer out of the fridge and switch on the television to relax in front of the fun and games they put on?

Our factory roof was leaking. It was in a sorry state, covered in patches and makeshift repairs. I spent the summer in the office leafing through specialist architecture magazines then, one idea leading to another, I came across a book about green roofs, or roofs covered in plants. I looked into the idea.

I spoke to a colleague about it and she contacted the local water agency to find out their forecasts for our region. A knowledgeable specialist came to explain the cycle and treatment of rain water. Finally, we decided to renovate the building and cover the new roof with plants that retain water and return it to the atmosphere by way of evapotranspiration (ET). The result of this is less water in the system in times of heavy rain. Another result is more effective insulation, protecting us from changes in temperature and absorbing noise. And of course, there is the added benefit of the pollinating insects which are returning to our site, the renewal of a little area of biodiversity and, to cap it all, we collect the surplus rainwater in tanks. We are self-sustaining in terms of water supply.

And two years later, these micro actions mean that we hardly use any more tap water, just a few litres to wash our hands and have a shower. All of our waste water is filtered in our natural water-treatment plant – a bamboo plantation. You'll find details of this, and other examples, later in the book.

I want to stress this: it is possible to reduce our local consumption of water in order to make a contribution on a larger scale. Yes, we can achieve what we wish for! It is within our scope, within the scope of our intelligence.

This is so much the case that several of my colleagues have adopted these techniques at home. They've installed solar panels, green roofs, beehives, bamboo for water treatment and underground water supply tanks. Not to mention car-sharing schemes to reduce their carbon footprint and cut fuel and maintenance costs for their cars. Yet another instance of micro action hitting the bullseye!

The answers are not always spectacular. It often takes a series of micro actions working together, taking effect in the medium and long term. Indeed, a visitor asked me what relation there was between Pocheco, where we make ecovelopes for automatic insertion, and Pocheco Canopée Conseil, our eco*lo*nomy consultancy business. I explained the connection between these two apparently distant professional worlds by saying that closely observing the sustainable management of certain north-European forests in the late 1990s had helped me unravel the threads of my own business: I first chose the paper mill, then the producers of ink and glue.

Whether it's products, processes or buildings, either upstream or downstream of our business activity, our team and their many micro teams constantly adhere to our three criteria for investment and this effective investment delivers measureable and highly encouraging results. We are able to offer these logical solutions to new customers and partners within the framework of the diversification of our business activity.

We accept our responsibilities. Solutions exist and we can implement them. Easily, economically and with public spirit!

When the word 'entrepreneur' takes on its full meaning

Entrepreneur, enterprise, enterprising... not words to be taken lightly! We have set up our consultancy in 'industrial eco*lo*nomy' because the solutions we have tried and tested have brought about substantial improvements in profitability, making working conditions less difficult and reducing the environmental impact of our business activities. We have tried them out ourselves, so they can be used by others. And for people without the resources of a company behind them, but who wish to act, we have also launched a non-profit organisation called la Maison de l'écolonomie (the Eco*lo*nomy Centre).

Many of the people who come to us for consultancy have already begun thinking about their own company's 'ecosystem'. For a long time, they may have been facing the same worries, doubts or dead-ends as us when it comes to environmental and social deterioration. If they *do* try to take action, they are often unable to see their plans through – whether that's because they're under pressure from shareholders reluctant to invest for medium- or long-term returns, or simply because of pressure in their own hectic lives. We help them. We bring together the different talents in their companies. On the way, we learn a lot and we share what we know. All in all, we are constantly rediscovering the energy of group work, spurred on by the urgency of the situation and by our involvement as citizens.

What a pleasure it is to find that the financial profitability of your company, at the service of the common good, is part of a virtuous circle that increases profits even further! We have so often been told the opposite. It has been drummed into us that green solutions are 20% more expensive than conventional ones. Maybe we have even started to believe it!

But doing business ecologically is not more expensive! What *does* cost more is doing things in a rush and without preparation; scraping savings here and there without taking stock, without thought, courage or ingenuity. Ignoring an idea is costly. As is not taking the time to chew a new idea over, when sleeping on it may be all that's needed.

But let's come back to profitability. Eco*lo*nomy improves profitability. Our company is no different from thousands of others. As the entrepreneur leading our set-up, I manage a team and keep a lid on expenses. Being directly answerable for our results, we find the 'eco*lo*nomical' method reconciles what was once irreconcilable, putting things back on an even keel, reintroducing common sense.

Things can be very different for big firms, whose directors are often out of touch with daily reality. But our approach is gaining public support, thanks to our low environmental impact, our reforestation programme and the open days we regularly hold. We live in harmony with our neighbours in the village. We are building the industry of the 21st century – a (circular) industry that will help put right the errors made during the industrial revolutions of previous centuries.

The company: a realm of possibilities

In the course of my professional life, I have been involved in six teams, all working on very different projects. I think I must have come up against every form of resistance imaginable over these twenty or so years. I'm happy to say that my current team, who have been together for about fifteen years, match what I have always dreamt of. They are easy-going, honest and thorough professionals, much more demanding on themselves than they are on others. They are responsible and profoundly fair people.

We have come a long way! All sorts of bad faith and pig-headedness blighted the initial period. There was little doubt that no one wanted me directing the company. Except, maybe (I have since found out), a silent majority that I became aware of once the early troubles had died down.

One example, among others, made an impression on me. This was a manager with a grand title that the previous directors had given her before I took over: I would have to think twice before getting rid of her (she admitted so herself!). She patiently listened to me questioning, thinking, suggesting and trying to convince, and then explained how and why what I was asking or suggesting could not be done. I began to wonder whether the previous shareholders had made the wrong choice and whether this woman should have been put in charge instead of me.

In the end, I had no choice but to let her go. Looking back on it now, I am still delighted with that decision. What a relief it is to be rid of those who vote against your original suggestion even before you have finished making it, and then to get together with those who are prepared to work with you and give things a try.

I notice, however, that many professionals base their power on saying no. It appears that taking time to explain how change cannot be implemented, rather than putting thought into some more original way forward, is more natural to many people today. I find this extremely frustrating.

I could have given up, but then I would have missed out on our current projects.

I opted for change and movement and I take responsibility for it. I make decisions by listening, reflecting, discussing, rectifying, chewing an idea over for twenty-four hours, asking for more information and then making my mind up. This must and can be done quickly. Whatever the issue, it's rarely advisable to dilly-dally or hesitate – that usually makes things worse or simply means you give up.

The workplace, its organisation and its architecture are enhanced by what goes on within its walls but also stand as sources of inspiration and add much to the meaning of the work that takes place there. This is how we consider the Pocheco site. The French singer Barbara, answering a journalist's questions about the familiar objects in her life, said, "My piano is not an object, my piano is a piano". In the same way, Pocheco is not a factory, Pocheco is Pocheco. In other words, it is a place which has meaning and which means something because of the talents and ideas present in it and the business projects under way in it.

The company, the place where we do business, has become a realm of possibilities. A creative melting pot of expertise and talent. This is what we achieve after introducing symmetry between financial economy, social contact and environmental economy. Growth at any price is replaced by the discipline of achieving balance and being self-financing. We did not allow capital, patiently accumulated by the company, its customers and its employees, to be squandered by and on an 'elite' minority. On the contrary, we maintain a steady stream of income and cash, which allows us to keep going.

We have pooled expertise and enriched knowledge with a return to the fair and healthy values of esteem and mutual respect. In this way, our energies are dedicated to eco*lo*nomy, the continuous reduction of the impact our activities have on the environment.

Putting eco*lo*nomy to the test

Trials and tribulations show us what we are capable of. The 2011-12 financial year was paradoxical for us. On the one hand, we were awarded a dozen prizes by public and private organisations. These prizes were the endorsement of our team's commitment to sustainable solutions in matters of social relations and environmental and financial management. On the other hand, a fire raged through our two product warehouses on the evening of 25th November 2011 and put our system severely to the test.

As soon as the afternoon shift realised they couldn't control the fire themselves, they proceeded to evacuate the building, which took 25 seconds for the whole 13,000m² area.

Our on-site insulation programme will soon allow us to eliminate the use of gas for heating completely, but we were still using it then. We were strengthening the warehouse roof and were just a week away from finishing the job when the fire broke out.

Our fire drill involves evacuating the premises with each team of workers, three or four times per year. The fire brigade works with us and we follow their guidance to the letter. They are familiar with the premises and are informed of every modification we make to our layout or organisation. Their last working visit had taken place less than four months previously.

We hold quality certifications covering both safety and environmental matters and our premises are never cluttered with equipment or anything that might hinder movement. Everything is in order outside as well. All areas are monitored, nothing is left to pile up hazardously and there is no litter anywhere. Nevertheless, teams from six different fire stations were called in: around a hundred well-trained, brave, organised and approachable individuals. They brought the fire under control in an hour and a half. They were then able to tell me that our industrial machinery had been saved in its entirety.

Our team flew into action like never before – or, perhaps, as always! We spent the weekend taking care of urgent matters and informing customers, who demonstrated remarkable composure. None of them flinched and they all assured us of their support. Not one delivery went out late.

Members of staff with families voluntarily in tow turned up on the Saturday morning and production was soon under way again twelve hours ahead of schedule. The factory was back in action at 11pm on the Sunday evening.

Right from the Saturday morning, Pocheco's suppliers of raw materials offered their support. I'm sure this can be traced back to the fact that we treat them with respect, even when we're negotiating with them on price.

Villagers living around the site, as well as council workers, shaken as they all were, also came to lend a hand from the outset.

We were asked to the town hall a few days later to give an update on the situation. The hall was packed. The villagers were right behind us. They were concentrated, constructive and united. One of them, whose house adjoins our premises, told me that he knew there was no danger, given that Pocheco uses no solvents, chemicals, little plastic and that, in short, the company works ecologically.

It would be untrue to say that coping with this catastrophe was simple. But the implementation of eco*lo*nomic principles over the last fifteen years made the work much easier, because those principles enabled us to organise ourselves.

We will, of course, rebuild. The plan for a new warehouse will have to incorporate improvements, so that the fire leaves something more than bitterness in its wake and takes us a step further forward.

What was left from the fire was sorted through with a fine-toothed comb and the remains were systematically recycled within four weeks. With the fire brigade's help, we measured toxicity of the air during the blaze and of the water used to put it out. Nothing abnormal was observed. Only the COD (chemical oxygen demand) was ten times higher than acceptable levels, which was due to an extinguishing agent, used during the first minutes, which starves the fire of oxygen. This meant runoff water had to be pumped out and recycled. The decision we made to manufacture our envelopes without dangerous substances (whenever humanly possible) was undoubtedly a factor in limiting the effects of this incident.

In our company, eco*lo*nomy is more than a way of working. It is a fair and reasonable management technique. First, it contributes to team spirit and, secondly, helps us pick ourselves up after traumas.

We are all thoroughly convinced of that now.

Chapter 4

Acting for sustainable development

To make development sustainable, we have to balance the environmental impact of a business, its impact on people and on finances. It goes without saying that a company which gives absolute priority to short-term financial profitability does not achieve such a balance. This short-term approach has, however, become the golden rule for the vast majority of financial investors.

If the profitability of an investment is all that counts and, moreover, a very short-term result is expected, then hasty methods become the norm.

In industry as a whole, cost-cutting takes priority over all other economic strategies. For instance, improving product durability is not judged to be appropriate. On the contrary, R&D departments programme the obsolescence of their products in order to limit their life span and ensure their rapid replacement. Neither is safeguarding jobs on the list – businesses are quick to relocate in search of low-cost labour. Another example is the development of international transport networks, increasing the distance between the object produced and its final recipient. The negative impact these so-called 'financial rationalisation' practices have on jobs and the environment is exponential.

The consequences of these ways of working on our society can be seen very clearly. We have unemployment, job insecurity, increased social inequality, reduced public funding, clogged transport systems, over-consumption of natural resources and uncontrolled expansion of volumes of waste.

Luckily, a growing section of the population is becoming aware of the harmful effects this degradation is having. But the vast majority of companies and directors completely ignore them.

We can observe, in passing, that in the industrial sector, even more than elsewhere, people who highlight these dramatic excesses are often still seen as unrealistic utopians or dangerous left-wing eco-loonies. This while the sorcerer's apprentices of high finance and big business, such as the late Steve Jobs or the honoured Bill Gates, are considered brilliant and efficient heroes.

When will they really bother to work out the impact that the exponential development of their technologies is having on society? And when will they encourage their shareholders to take this impact into account? When will they opt to dedicate part of their resources to the research and development of a sustainable model, really sustainable as regards human activity and natural resources as well as energy and raw materials?

Sustainable development, as long as it doesn't become just a marketing tool, is a way of working and researching that enables companies to offer innovative solutions without any drop in profitability.

In short, sustainable development allows us to manufacture and do business differently and is not limited to an elite few companies. The proof of this is that Pocheco's own current good health is grounded in sustainable development, however demanding the context might be. Doing business differently is taking the simple option of finding a balance between values and resources. In concrete terms, doing business differently is making sure that, with each investment, the expected result brings about a noticeable and measurable reduction in the impact of our activity on the environment, as well as a decrease in risks and stress in the workplace. All this accompanied by an increase in productivity.

Reducing environmental impact

Environmental impact must be dealt with from the outset in any project. It's important and realistic, in the medium and long term, to consider carefully the resources that will be needed. They're exhaustible and any project must be thought through with this in mind.

Recycling, as long as it is efficient, affords a considerable reduction in our depletion of natural resources. This is because it produces reusable waste, thereby lengthening the life span of raw materials.

Recycling must be seen as a priority resource. If this resource is the fruit of waste collection and transformation, then two birds can be killed with one stone: we avoid the dispersal of waste and reduce the amount of resources taken from the environment.

To achieve this, priority must be given (and this may be the role of public authorities) to the collection and recycling of waste. We could set up treatment and recycling works near waste plants to transform this waste into new resources. Centres taking part in the 'virtuous cycle' of re-use could be established.

Taking the example of Pocheco's envelopes, paper is a reusable resource. When collected as waste, it can be sent to produce cardboard for packaging or furnishings and it can even be used as insulation. Moreover, knowing that our products come from responsibly managed forests (for each tree cut down, three are planted, see Chapter 5), it contributes to the increase in forested areas and helps to reduce the quantity of CO_2 in the Earth's atmosphere.

Recovering waste locally opens the door to new work opportunities. It plays a part in the development of local employment and reduces the need for people to travel long distances to get to work. It also means transporting raw materials over shorter distances. The development of medium-sized treatment and recycling units is very promising and it would be appropriate to roll them out widely.

Although many in industrial and political circles insist that this programme is unrealistic or utopian, we can see that this model, with multiple, smaller treatment and recycling units, calls into question the model pursued by the large corporations. In order to globalise their development, they propound only the virtues of gigantism.

To sum up, the subject of the environmental impact of our activities challenges the existing model and calls for its far-reaching reform. At Pocheco, we do not restrict ourselves to meeting the various regulatory requirements; we constantly seek to improve ourselves and limit our environmental impact ever further.

The over-centralisation of energy production must also be challenged. On this point, the development of local production sources is a solution. Let us not forget that the total yearly energy needs of the world's population could be met with the energy produced in one hour of sunshine,[1] if we could find and implement the means of harnessing and transforming this energy.

---

1. Source: *Nature*, 443, 19-22 (7th September 2006).

As regards housing, we can see that current domestic construction techniques are beginning to have an impact. The same results are possible commercially and industrially, if we so decide. Even though much more work is still needed.

From this point of view, we must resist the argument that decries new energy sources on the grounds that they cost the end-user too much. For example, nuclear power is and has always been subsidised by the public authorities in France (and elsewhere in the West) and so, indirectly, by all citizens. In 2012, our bills did not, therefore, reflect the real price of electricity generated by nuclear power. Far from it.

Improving working conditions

The second part of sustainable development concerns working conditions.

Modernisation of equipment in the workplace must not be carried out to the detriment of jobs and employees. When all's said and done, who are we working for? What meaning do we give to work? What are the products that we make intended for: to increase the wealth of a select few or to improve the well-being of the majority? We should always bear in mind the link between what we are manufacturing, who it's for and why we are making it.

The rules of sustainable development encompass the notion of improving working conditions and rightly so. It should be a constant concern. How could you be happy knowing your tablet or PC has been produced at the cost of human exhaustion? What madness leads us to take such little account of this reality?

In our factory, we believe that repetitive and arduous tasks, for example those causing premature wear to the skeleton, should be automated. This is in order to give free rein to people's energy and put it to more intelligent use – the intelligence of non-repetitive physical movement or purely intellectual activity. I make no distinction between these two points as regards their usefulness. By automating the most physically demanding jobs, we have freed-up time for developing the quality (and ensuring the quality control) of our production processes. We have rationalised our processes and improved performance by reducing waste, for example. The result is increased satisfaction among our customers who have, in turn, become more loyal to us.

Another outcome is better organisation of our work, enabling us to devote around 30% of our time to sharing knowledge and improving our performance.

We have also achieved significant and long-lasting reductions in production costs, all by excluding waste. Indeed, our teams are under less stress and less exhausted, our colleagues suffer fewer injuries and, therefore, take less time off sick. In these circumstances, productivity grows rapidly and, along with it, so does business profitability.

By reducing the difficult and/or dangerous nature of our work, we provide safe conditions for our employees to work in, all the while protecting their jobs. Here, we have another example of good management decisions and not of utopian thinking. Choices like these are within the reach of any business owner who cares to give them some thought. But it does all presuppose, however, that one accepts the idea of change.

This, in turn, simply requires that people free themselves collectively from out-of-date thinking and habits. All too often we find ourselves in a dead end, facing assertions such as, "I've always done it like that!" – and you're as likely to hear these words in a board meeting as on the shopfloor. It is this deadening mixture of lack of imagination, intellectual ossification and fear of the unknown that hinders the progress of sustainable development.

Change, imagination and creativity can neither be imposed nor improvised. Time and a great deal of pragmatism are needed. A lot of perseverance too, and forget any idea that, just by setting the cat among the pigeons, we can sort everything out. This can only be achieved slowly but surely through constant work, not in fits and starts. That, in turn, takes financial resources.

Improving productivity

Obviously, any changes adopted within a sustainable development plan contain a financial element, looking for an eventual return on investment even if they don't deliver an immediate profit. But, on the whole, it is the nature of industry to tie sums of money up for long periods. We need to be aware that industry works over long time spans.

A plan can only be drawn up and implemented if there are a number of years ahead in which to carry it out. Why do people try to force industry into the short time spans which are the norm in service companies? Services rely on fewer materials and equipment, therefore tying-up less money.

I stress the complementarity of services and industry within an economy, precisely because I believe it is good management practice to balance out long-term activities with short-term ones. Once again, attempting to apply the rules of immediate profit to all kinds of business activities has given rise to damaging business practices (like relocation to reduce labour costs).

Sustainable development accepts that several different economic models can complement each other. In other words, our thinking should vary depending on whether we are supplying a service or a product.

Whereas companies generally consider that practices that respect ecology and the environment are additional burdens which lower productivity, at Pocheco productivity actually increased while we were implementing them. We reduced our environmental impact by promoting the circular economy and made jobs less strenuous by fostering better use of human intelligence.

Gains in productivity can neither be achieved by neglecting regular renewal and overhaul of machinery, nor by reducing spending on preventive maintenance. The opposite is true, in fact. So as to improve the quality of our services, we invest 10% of our annual turnover in the continuous modernisation of our equipment, in search of sustainable materials and in lifelong learning.

Beware of greenwashing

What is known as greenwashing is a caricature of what I have just described. Applied to an organisation or company, it means emphasising the best-looking elements of sustainable development without making any significant changes to behaviour or business methods.

Greenwashing, then, is a trick by which a product, company or process is made to look sustainable even though it has a negative impact on natural resources and the ecological or human environment.

The only way of knowing if a company or group uses greenwashing, or not, is to go into their working methods in detail. It's easy to spot if these methods are opaque or ambiguous. I remember a documentary about a company in Silicon Valley, where a great deal was made of their electric shuttle for visitors and the paper cups in their coffee machine. But, following the report, it became clear that this same company operated an ocean of extremely powerful servers, consuming mind-boggling amounts of energy and giving off such levels of heat that they had to be cooled, otherwise everything would catch fire. There was no indication as to the impact of this. This is typical greenwashing, bringing the customer to visit in an electric shuttle and serving coffee in paper cups but, behind the scenes, consuming enormous quantities of energy with a singular lack of transparency.

Because companies are caught between managing their 'general public' image (often connected to the sale of products intended for this general public) and stringent regulations, including their overriding obligation to pay shareholders and/or middlemen, they choose to highlight only selected aspects of their work, most often by way of expensive communication campaigns.

This can happen even in the best cases. Such companies resort to greenwashing only in emergencies. They feel the need to appear more virtuous than is really the case. Actually, this betrays the initial stages of an important and deep-rooted process which will need time to mature. They may come to realise that the benefits of a truly ecological policy outweigh those of greenwashing.

I have seen impressive developments with certain major customers over fifteen years. Constant effort by their teams has helped them break free from the caricature and modify their methods and reasoning in depth. This has boosted the well-being of all and worked to everyone's benefit.

In my own profession, I have seen this work carried out by a large Scandinavian paper manufacturer. The company realised what a disastrous effect its actions in the 1970s had on the environment, hence on its brand image, and decided to go back to basics in its business. It began by learning all over again how to manage its forestry resources, then how to reduce energy consumption in its transformation processes (for example, by using forestry waste to heat water). It also replaced harmful products and carefully supervised its water consumption and reprocessing.

Since the early years of this century, it has faced financial constraints linked to the global development of its activities. It is not, as yet, benefitting fully from the virtuous circle it has entered, but I think it's only a question of time.

Sustainable development does not solve the problem of global competition. When faced with less scrupulous rivals, in the name of 'sacrosanct' freedom of trade and international competition, large companies must also overhaul their business model in detail.

This may explain why a majority of global companies use communication ploys to greenwash their production methods, in this case with total cynicism and lack of integrity.

But the correct verdict will be delivered, if one believes, as I do, that natural resources *and* people are nearing exhaustion and that, sooner or later, the truth will out.

PART TWO

Practising What We Preach

"It is cheaper to produce ecologically!"

As our company is our major testing ground and the examples I draw on in this text are taken from its history, I would first like to say a few words about what we do.

Our SME was founded in 1928 and produces 'transactional' envelopes, which are used to send bank statements, health insurance and unemployment benefit account statements and energy and telephone bills to millions of customers. Our clients are large national and European operators and are either public, semi-public or private. They have service relationships with individual customers and companies.

They communicate with their customers in various ways, the most frequent of which is the letter, sent by post in a paper envelope. This means of communication is still far more popular than the Internet for our customers.

The Pocheco team is made up of 114 employees specialising in the industrial production of transactional envelopes suitable for automatic insertion machinery. Seven team leaders coordinate the production work. The maintenance, logistics, quality control and sales administration teams spare no effort in ensuring that our production processes run smoothly and that the quality of our products lives up to our commitment and our customers' expectations. A few people take care of the administrative work. And our management committee is made up of six people (three women and three men) who have been coordinating our teams for the past ten years. They all come from different geographical, social and training backgrounds.

When visitors come to our factory, they are often surprised to discover that making an envelope requires a level of expertise and a combination of technologies that they would not have imagined beforehand. This is quite understandable. After all, the envelope is the first part of the letter that we throw away, because of course we are far more interested in the important information contained, for example, in the bank statement or mobile phone bill. Basically, we only worry about the envelope if there is something wrong with it, if it arrives already open for instance.

As you can see, the activity (envelope manufacturing) on which we base our sustainable development experiments is so run-of-the-mill that our suggestions can easily be applied to other industries. Especially as our product costs next to nothing, particularly when compared to the overall cost of producing and sending large quantities of letters.

Profitability in this industrial activity is well within the norms of industry in general. Heavy investment is needed to equip a site like ours with material to produce two billion envelopes a year. Initial outlay is about €20 million with return on investment achieved in more than fifteen years. It could be said that the paltry value of an individual envelope is as insignificant as the correlated investments and loan repayments are burdensome. I do not write this to discourage investors, but rather to highlight a paradox.

Our research in the area of sustainable development has not arisen from boredom at working in such a profitable business that we do not know what to come up with next to occupy our minds! Sustainable development and the working methods we associate with it are, quite frankly, a beneficial source of productivity.

Our industrial activity is not linked directly to questions of environmental management. However, as with any human activity, it has an impact on the environment – in fact, multiple impacts on the environment. This comes into play right from the start with our choice of our raw materials.

Chapter 5

Raw materials: leaving nothing to chance

At Pocheco, we are committed to our product promise. In other words, supplying paper envelopes to our key-account customers whose computerised data management centres process, prepare and send tens or hundreds of thousands of letters to their millions of customers.

These envelopes are fed through automatic machines which collect data and check its accuracy (so that your bank statement is not sent to your neighbour, for instance). An envelope's mechanographic qualities must be assured upstream of manufacturing, so as to ensure that it arrives at the correct destination while maintaining the confidentiality of the letter it contains. The chosen paper has to undergo and withstand mechanical processing and the ink selected must allow for easy reading and comply with the organisation's corporate identity. We need to keep our promises to customers, naturally, but respect the environment as well.

When I took over the company, one of my first steps was to check on where the raw materials came from, because reducing the environmental impact of our activity was not limited to the production processes of the company. Upstream, we also had to analyse all raw materials. Paper, ink, glue and the material used for the windows were all scrutinised most attentively.

Where does the wood used to make our paper come from?

At Pocheco, 50% of the price of an envelope goes on paper, our main raw material. And so it was a logical first step to look into the quality and production methods of the paper we use.

When I started working at Pocheco, I was convinced that using paper destroyed forests, which worried me. I thought that Pocheco, which at the time transformed 5 or 6 thousand tonnes of paper into about 850 million envelopes a year, would be an interesting company to manage. The problem was that if we were killing a tree for every 1,000 envelopes we made, then things had to change. I made enquiries and met paper manufacturers. I found one in Finland (UPM) which, without shouting about it, had introduced extremely positive procedures for increasing the surface area of local forests. In other words, for every tree felled, it systematically planted three others, all with minimum fuss and without anyone knowing. It was simply because its original business had been forest management. Forests are maintained by thinning, or clearing away vegetation around particular trees deemed capable of many years' growth, so as to leave them sufficient space. The strongest and straightest specimens are left to grow for making furniture. And when trees are replanted, care is taken to preserve the biodiversity of the forests. It is not enough to grow only one species in an area, a variety of local species must be planted in order to develop biodiversity.

This sustainable management is backed up by a tracking system which guarantees the viability of these methods as long-term solutions. The felling machine selects trees to be cut down using satellite technology. I was fascinated by these felling machines when I saw them. Machines on caterpillar tracks can crush new shoots and so this paper manufacturer uses machines on stilts which spare the shoots and which, better still, run on a biofuel made from organic material, woodchips for instance. I found this very reassuring.

The forest managed by the company extends about a hundred kilometres around the paper mill, thereby proportionately reducing the impact of transport. It has also introduced ISO certification for consumption of water and chemicals in the mill. You may or may not know that water is needed to manufacture paper. Paper pulp is diluted in water so that the fibres come to the surface. The solution is then sprayed onto a cloth to guide the fibres in a certain direction. This produces paper with mechanical and graphic qualities which depend on the direction of the fibres. Chemicals are also added and make all the difference to the composition of the paper and the skill with which it is manufactured.

This particular paper-maker took water from the environment and transformed the paper, first by spraying then by drying. During the drying stage, it collected 95% of the water used in the form of steam, which was then returned to a liquid state full of chemicals. Not very dangerous ones, because no optical brighteners[1] or other dangerously polluting chemicals remained, but chalk all the same, along with other elements. So it installed a water-treatment plant nearby from which the water emerges so clean that it is inert and free from bacteria. It then adds bacteria once more and brings the water down to the ambient temperature before putting it back into the environment, as clean and 'alive' as it was when it entered the mill. With reduction of water and energy consumption being an important criterion, it set about halving its use of both within fifteen years. It took its water from the environment and only put it back once it had been cleansed.

Seeing the work carried out by this expert paper-maker, we decided to buy 100% of our paper from them, and this is still the case today. Thanks to this, we have the guarantee that Pocheco is participating in increasing European forestry cover and respecting species biodiversity.

This enables me to lay to rest myths about sustainable forestry that have been so widely circulated that they are generally believed. In fact, in the conditions described here, the manufacture and use of paper allow commercially managed forests to increase in surface area. Three trees planted for every tree felled to manufacture our paper makes a big difference! It's an extremely positive practice for the air we breathe, because a tree actually consumes the most CO_2 during the first ten years of its life. Each year, Pocheco plays a part in planting 180,000 trees in this manner. By choosing our envelopes, our customers become partners in this virtuous action.

An example: one of our ecovelopes has been a runaway success. It's based on cutting-edge research. The paper is made exclusively from sawdust from sawmills. The forest is cultivated and select trees are felled to make beams or wood for joinery. The shavings are collected and directly transformed into paper pulp. This pulp is not whitened, which gives the envelope its natural, vanilla colour, which customers like. This simplified process saves considerably on the quantities of water and energy needed in its manufacture.

What's more, its texture and strength are such that we have been able to lower the weight (measured in grams per square metre – gsm)

---

1. Optical brighteners are synthetic organic molecules which absorb ultraviolet rays and emit this energy in visible form by fluorescence. They are used by industry to whiten materials which tend to turn yellow.

of the paper used. We have called this envelope Oxymore.[2] An Oxymore envelope made from 75gsm paper offers the same characteristics as a 'normal' white envelope made from 80gsm paper. Here again, it's a question of consuming fewer raw materials. Consuming less and better. If we take the example of telecoms company SFR, this represents a saving of 50 tonnes of paper for 145 million envelopes used yearly.

All things considered, the production of an Oxymore envelope releases 30% less CO_2 than that of a normal envelope, in itself far less polluting than an e-mail! And today, thanks to the choice made by our key-account customers, 14% of the envelopes we manufacture are Oxymore.

Finally, we have given preference to envelope windows that are themselves made out of paper (a translucent paper, slightly less transparent than a plastic window), not out of PVC or PET, precisely because these could not be thrown into the bin and recycled.

For all these reasons and, contrary to what we so often hear, paper envelopes are good for the environment!

What about inks and glues?

Our aim is to constantly eliminate more of the toxic products our inks may contain – solvents and chemical molecules carrying volatile organic components (VOCs) – so as to reduce their impact on the environment. At the same time, and this is not a mere detail, it allows us to reduce the difficulty and danger of working with inks. Lastly, it facilitates the recycling process, often bringing about a reduction in expenses and purchasing costs.

For an envelope to be certified 'NF-Environnement' (an environmental certification standard), its ink must contain less than 5% of residual VOCs. Ours contain less than 2%: we are well within the legal limits. It's a matter of protecting our customers, their customers

---

2. At Pocheco, we name our products after literary terms – for instance, the Oxymore (from the Greek oxymoron). An oxymoron is an expression which, by combining two contradictory concepts, creates a different and often paradoxical meaning: fully empty, white night or... English cooking! For a long time, people said using paper destroyed forests but, with our ecovelopes, exactly the opposite happens. An oxymoron in itself!

and the workers at Pocheco. Visitors to our factory immediately notice that no smell of printing solvent bothers them. Quite right, because we don't use any!

The pigments in our inks are natural and diluted in water, which makes them easy to recycle. We mix them ourselves to obtain our colours, thanks to our new semi-automatic mixing station, which creates exact colours in exact quantities.

We have contracts with well-known companies to collect our ink vats, much the same as for our waste paper or the plastic from our pallets. This requires us to sort the vats prior to collection, using specially adapted containers.

Once our ink vats have been emptied, we clean them with a formula similar to standard household soap. The dirty water is then kept in a tank without needing any further treatment. It is collected every six weeks for use by a local cement works.

As for our glues, you could eat them! They are water-based and, as with our inks, our suppliers agreed to modify their formula and exclude solvents, heavy metals and VOCs. The regulatory standard imposes a maximum of 2% VOCs but they contain none at all.

The transport question

Finally, and still with the same objective of reducing our environmental impact, we must also take care with the way materials are transported to our factory. We mostly use local companies but, in some cases we work with companies located 2,000km away, such as our Finnish paper-maker. In these cases, we favour wherever possible forms of transport with a low carbon footprint, meaning rail or ship, rather than road transport which is much less 'clean'.

Each step upstream of our manufacturing process has been thought out so as to reduce our carbon footprint. Where solutions do not exist yet, we can suggest them. One of the strong points of sustainable development certainly lies in the evolutionary nature of its solutions. What doesn't exist today will certainly be invented tomorrow, according to the well-known principle of continuous improvement.

Theme 1: Raw material management

Raw materials	Initial Cost	Annual Cost	Notes	Early[3] Eco*lon*omies	Eco*lon*omies/yr[4] € and equivalent CO$_2$ (CO$_2$e)		Notes
Paper from sustainably managed forests and certification (1997)	€0	€12,000	Annual cost of certification	€0	€0	558,600,000kg CO$_2$e	94% of our paper is PEFC certified and 6% is FSC – forests are managed with respect for biodiversity and social conditions.
Use of paper window film instead of plastic (2000)	€15,000	€0	Cost includes testing in our factory and mailrooms.	€540,000	€0	700,000kg CO$_2$e	85% of products are made with paper window film.
Elimination of solvent-based inks (2000)	€25,000	€0	Cost includes test period and machine down time.	€450,000	€220,000	36,000kg CO$_2$e	These inks use larger containers, are cheaper, reduce hazards. Don't need a fire proof room.
Fewer toxic products used on site (2002)	€10,000	€0		€0	€3,000		Suppression of ATEX zone and fewer risks on site.
Creation of 'Oxymore' envelope (2008)	€15,000	€0	Machine tests, marketing costs.	€0	€19,000	416,000kg CO$_2$e	Oxymore is lighter, costs customers less and has 30% lower carbon footprint – saving 600+ tonnes of paper since 2008.
'Tornado' packaging system (1999)	€1,500,000	€50,000	Buying new technology and regular purchase and maintenance of equipment.	€0	€90,000	24,000kg CO$_2$e	No boxes, pallets, plastic. Reusable and returnable. No manual handling. Less work-related illness. Customer loyalty. Increased productivity.
'Letterbox' packaging system (2012)	€172,000	€0	Purchase of Letterboxes.	€0	€6,500	6,400kg CO$_2$e	Reusable crates. No more plastic. Stackable boxes save space and reduce transport costs.
TOTAL	€1,737,000	€62,000		€990,000	€338,500	559,782,400kg CO$_2$e	
Return on investment	6.3 years						

---

3. Eco*lon*omies made at the beginning of 2000 and over three years.

4. Eco*lon*omies made since 2003, every year.

Chapter 6

Eco*lo*nomy and life cycle assessment (not as bad as it sounds)

In today's economy-driven world, the notion of productivity is linked to that of speed. However, eco*lo*nomy teaches us to treat time as an ally, even if it means spending a little – or a lot – of it working out all aspects of an operation before launching it. First, statutory changes need to be anticipated, then information must be collected at source. The final step is taking time – again, sometimes lots of it – to analyse the life cycle of products and weigh up their exact environmental impact.

At Pocheco, experience has shown that the more organised we are upstream, the lower the financial costs and risks of accidents or waste. The key word for us is anticipation which, in the end, leaves us time and space for the development of new projects.

Whenever possible, we apply rules and standards more firmly and strictly than officially required. This means we do not suffer unduly from statutory changes because we stay ahead of them. Over time I've found that taking the lead in these matters makes management easier, smoother and cheaper. In a similar vein, our suppliers have taken to proposing their own innovations spontaneously.

Finally, by planning carefully, we have reduced the comings and goings of lorries – for delivery and collection – by a third. The consequence is less carbon emitted, less work for the logistics team and better visibility in the workshop and stockroom. Hence, a lower risk of accidents on-site.

Time is an important factor. For instance, what we were worrying about yesterday while we were listening to the catastrophes and scaremongering on the television news cannot be solved by a good night's sleep. The problems are still there when we come into the office next morning, even if they have faded from the media spotlight. But being assaulted by bad news progressively numbs our individual ability to bounce back. Even so, I believe we can act individually. And that by increasing the number of initiatives we undertake and by joining together with others, we can make useful interventions. One change leads to the next and brick by brick, with time, everything changes.

This is only possible if everyone takes personal responsibility, takes an active part in collective action and, well-informed by a regularly updated life cycle, knows where to begin their task of rationalisation and reduction of impacts.

Checking our sources

If, at our own level, we wish to help re-establish a sustainable environment and society, we must begin by collecting precise and objective information. In other words, information which has not been manipulated by financial interests represented by lobby groups. A good example is the IT industry.

I meet many people who are surprised to learn that computers – for instance, the one I am writing this text on – and contemporary methods of sending messages – such as email – consume exponential quantities of raw materials and energy and cause massive amounts of waste when disposed of.[1] Jérôme Fenoglio explained it in an article in *le Monde* in June 2007:

> *"Computers are amongst the most inefficient devices ever invented"* writes the specialist Timothy Prickett Morgan. *Most of the electricity which powers the computer is lost through heat, noise and light. According to Urs Hölze, vice President of Google, "a computer wastes half of its energy and a server wastes a third."*[2]

Such expense went unnoticed for a long time in data processing centre budgets and energy consumption by those industries channelling our exchanges of digital data is still increasing exponentially, on a global level.

---

1. On this subject, see the life cycle assessment carried out by the Ademe and the Bio Intelligence Service consultancy, published in July 2011: *Analyse comparée des impacts environnementaux de la communication par voie électronique (Comparative analysis of impacts on the environment of electronic communication).* www.bit.ly/ecolonomy02

[2] To learn more, see: 'IT overheating alert': www.bit.ly/ecolonomy04

Why do you think that today's Web conglomerates – Google, Microsoft and Yahoo – try to build their factories, housing hundreds of thousands of servers and linked by optical fibre, so close to hydroelectric production sites? Because the laws of physics are beginning to catch up with this sector. Between 2000 and 2005, Fenoglio tells us in the same article, consumption of electricity by data centres doubled, reaching 45 billion kW/h and representing a yearly total of €6.5 billion globally. These figures have increased continuously up to the present day. The digital industry has become one of the biggest energy consumers in the world. Online information exchange, ever-increasing in number as paper information exchange decreases, can now be considered an aggravating factor in global warming.

I must also mention the material needed for IT data exchanges. According to the UN, personal computers, printers, servers, underwater cables and satellites are alone responsible for 40 million tonnes of non-recyclable and non-degradable waste each year. It is plain to see that, even if the 'dematerialisation' of mail and data exchanges is often evoked in everyday language, nothing is less immaterial than this industry!

Don't worry, I'm not suggesting a return to the horse and cart. Nor to quills and inkwells! But I would like people to stop burying their heads in the sand. I am one of those who think the truth is less complicated to face than imprecision. We waste a lot of time and energy lying to ourselves – beginning with the use of inappropriate terms and concepts, like 'dematerialisation' and 'virtual' which actually entail the use of large quantities of 'actual' materials and equipment.

During a conference in November 2007, while I was defending these arguments, a listener interrupted me, "What you say is astonishing, but can you prove it? Have you carried out an LCA?"

I gave two answers to this participant. First: does anyone ask IT companies who say 'dematerialisation' is good for the environment to prove it? Secondly: What is an LCA?

The life cycle assessment

An LCA is a life cycle assessment. This means applying a scientific method (if possible without deforming the data collected) to the precise evaluation of the environmental impact of the production of goods or services.

For instance, to produce paper envelopes we need wood, water and energy. Each step, before and after the production of an envelope, must be assessed. The benchmarks vary according to the activity under scrutiny. I decided to carry out an LCA at Pocheco. For the paper we use and its production, we examined ten criteria: air acidification, water acidification, water eutrophication,[3] destruction of the ozone layer, photochemical oxidation,[4] human toxicity, aquatic ecotoxicity, contribution to climate change, exhaustion of natural raw materials and energy consumption. A carbon footprint report completes the study.

In the course of doing this, we came across a thousand unresolved parameters and questions and we had to consult a global database called ECOINVENT, which was set up in 2003-2004 and is housed at the UN in New York.[5] Thanks to the centralisation and clustering of all the data from every LCA ever conducted, we can cross-check information and clarify results on practically any product. From a certain company size upwards, an LCA is mandatory. But many products still escape this process. This is regrettable when judged in the light of the expected exhaustion of certain raw materials. But that's another story.

When we launched this assessment at Pocheco, the idea was to evaluate the impact of our activities on the environment and to find out how to reduce our negative impact and improve our performance.

According to the results of our study, to date and in line with the criteria evaluated in our LCA, the paper envelope is less polluting than its virtual counterpart for conveying electronic information, the email. Of course, you will think that being an envelope manufacturer, I am bound to say this! Believe it or not, had the results not been in favour of paper mail, we would first have directed all our efforts into reducing our impact. If that had not been enough, we would have given ourselves five years to convert Pocheco to a less destructive activity. Because it

---

3. Development of surface algae exhausting the oxygen present in water.

4. 'Smog', nitrogen oxide acting as a catalyst in the chemistry of ozone. In small doses, it contributes to the destruction of ozone, but in larger quantities, it contributes to acid rain. Source : www.dictionnaire-environnement.com

5. www.ecoinvent.org

seems unthinkable, on the virtuous pretext of saving our jobs, to destroy our environment, and therefore the future, in the process.

And you will probably think that, as you already own a computer, the impacts are the same whether you consult your phone bill on it or not. But the LCA calculated the impacts for both scenarios: building and running the computer as well as the infrastructure needed to send the document by post (road, lorry, train, etc.) and those figures were then proportionally reduced to represent only those impacts generated for the specific document we were studying.

Incidentally, we had to laugh (so as not to cry) when we found out that computer manufacturers, the same people who encourage 'dematerialisation', 'e-billing' and 'paper-free communication' as if they were going out of fashion, had always avoided carrying out LCAs on their machines on the pretext that "a computer is made up of over 1500 parts and this rules out any assessment". The mind boggles...

The next thing is to ask about the reasons for this total opacity.

The Ademe and the Bio Intelligence Service consultancy, in their study *Comparative assessment of the environmental impact of communication by electronic means* published in July 2011, explain in the section headed 'Data sources' that "the collection of data not having been possible from sector players, essentially for reasons of confidentiality, all data needed for the modelling of the equipment through which information passes comes from extensive bibliographical research and a phase of exchanges with professionals from the sector".

We also came across this total opacity in our own LCA, but we worked through it because it seemed vital to assess seriously the impact of our electronic devices.

To conclude this anecdote, which in my opinion is highly revealing of the nervousness of large corporations, we produced this study thanks to a team of researchers from the CNRS. They patiently dismantled, weighed and listed all the components of a laptop computer. This meant that we produced the first LCA in the world for a laptop computer! Public services have a good side, especially when they give objective answers to big lobby groups.

Theme 2: Life Cycle Analysis

Comparative Life Cycle Analysis of a transactional document sent by post and by e-mail

May 2011

Method

A Life Cycle Analysis is a complete and complex analysis which exceeds, and yet includes, the carbon footprint issue. The impacts on the depletion of natural resources, air, water and human resources are also measured throughout the life cycle of a product. A specialised engineering firm has conducted a comparative Life Cycle Analysis of a management document sent, received, read and archived, by post and by e-mail.

The term transactional document includes invoices, account statements and status reports. In accordance with the ISO 14040 standard, this analysis has been validated by a group of independent experts.

The five stages of a Life Cycle Analysis

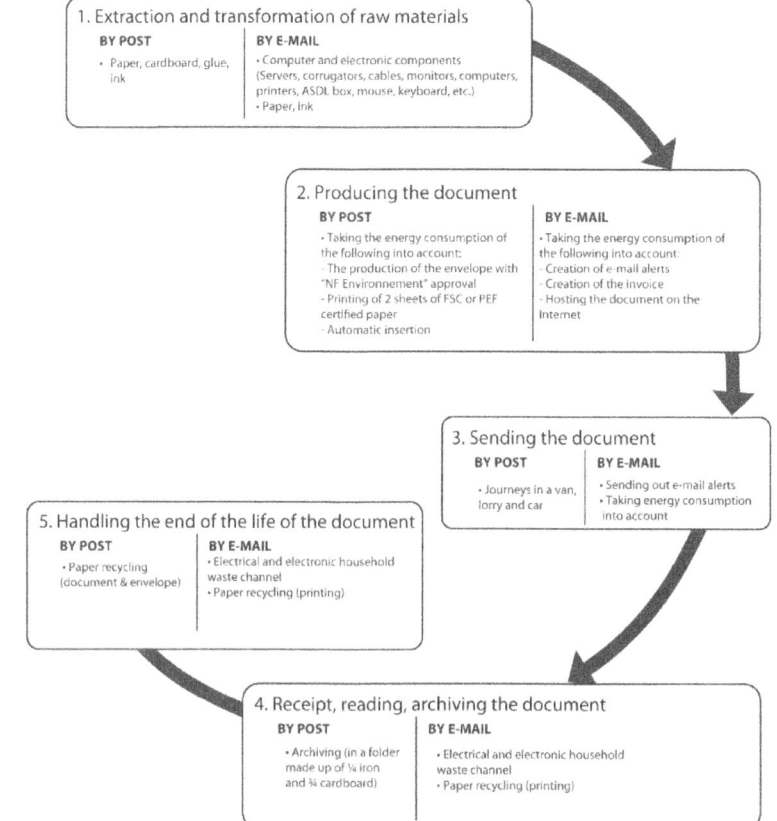

1. Extraction and transformation of raw materials
   - BY POST
     - Paper, cardboard, glue, ink
   - BY E-MAIL
     - Computer and electronic components (Servers, corrugators, cables, monitors, computers, printers, ADSL box, mouse, keyboard, etc.)
     - Paper, ink

2. Producing the document
   - BY POST
     - Taking the energy consumption of the following into account:
       - The production of the envelope with "NF Environnement" approval
       - Printing of 2 sheets of FSC or PEF certified paper
       - Automatic insertion
   - BY E-MAIL
     - Taking the energy consumption of the following into account:
       - Creation of e-mail alerts
       - Creation of the invoice
       - Hosting the document on the Internet

3. Sending the document
   - BY POST
     - Journeys in a van, lorry and car
   - BY E-MAIL
     - Sending out e-mail alerts
     - Taking energy consumption into account

4. Receipt, reading, archiving the document
   - BY POST
     - Archiving (in a folder made up of ¼ iron and ¾ cardboard)
   - BY E-MAIL
     - Electrical and electronic household waste channel
     - Paper recycling (printing)

5. Handling the end of the life of the document
   - BY POST
     - Paper recycling (document & envelope)
   - BY E-MAIL
     - Electrical and electronic household waste channel
     - Paper recycling (printing)

Doing Business and Manufacturing Differently

Modelling

Once collected, the data corresponding to each stage is modelled using software that measures the impact on ten environmental indicators. The paper document, for the basic case, is comprised of two A4 sheets, printed recto-verso (see stage 2 of the Five Stages of a Life Cycle Analysis).

As an example ...

The environmental impact of a digital document increases with the time spent on the Internet and the frequency of printing. Five assumptions have been established, by varying both of these criteria, between 1 and 30 minutes of reading, and between 0 and 100% for the printing rate.

To take one example from the five assumptions, by taking three minutes to read the document, and systematically printing out the document, we see that the digital document has more of an impact than the paper document, whatever the indicator selected.

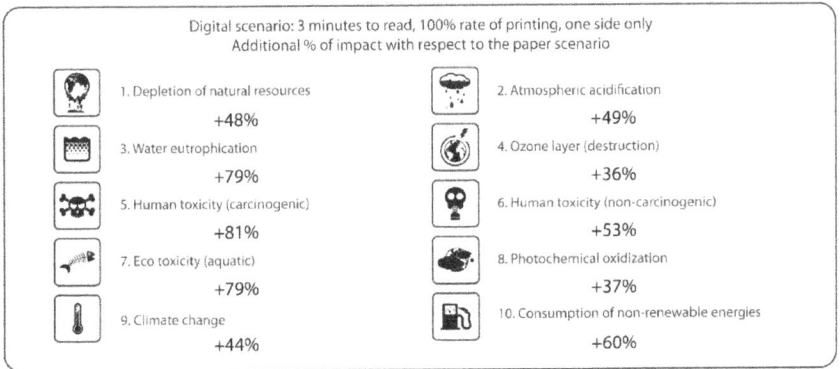

Digital scenario: 3 minutes to read, 100% rate of printing, one side only
Additional % of impact with respect to the paper scenario

1. Depletion of natural resources +48%
2. Atmospheric acidification +49%
3. Water eutrophication +79%
4. Ozone layer (destruction) +36%
5. Human toxicity (carcinogenic) +81%
6. Human toxicity (non-carcinogenic) +53%
7. Eco toxicity (aquatic) +79%
8. Photochemical oxidization +37%
9. Climate change +44%
10. Consumption of non-renewable energies +60%

Conclusions

· On the whole, a transactional document sent by e-mail creates more of an impact than the same document sent by post. The impacts of the life cycle of a digital transactional document depends considerably on the behaviour of the final customer receiving the document: time spent reading the document and the printing parameters.

· A paper document is systematically more advantageous than a digital document with regard to the water pollution indicators (eutrophication and aquatic Eco toxicity) and human toxicity (carcinogenic).

· In almost all cases when considering digital assumptions, a document sent by e-mail requires the consumption of more non-renewable energy than the paper scenario.

· In the paper scenario, two pages of the transactional document are at the origin of most environmental impacts (which is logical, as the sheets represent 75% of the envelope weight).

· As for the digital scenario, computing and printing represent the majority of the environmental impact.

Chapter 7

Managing energy, from the basement to the attic

In any company, energy management is a key job. All company directors will tell you the same thing, without really knowing much about improving energy efficiency and certainly not knowing about the most ecolonomic solutions. At Pocheco, all aspects of energy management, essential for company profitability, were examined and evaluated. We found ways, first to lower the energy consumption of our buildings, then of our production line and, finally, to diversify our energy sources.

Lowering consumption in the buildings

When we started our renovation work, we realised that if we tried to make only one clean energy production technique profitable, the return on investment would be slower than if we linked several techniques.

This is how we came to associate solar panels with the collection of rainwater from the roof, planting a living roof and façade, replacing as much artificial light as possible with natural light from outside and insulating the buildings.

For example, the workshops and storage areas at Pocheco cover 8,000m² of the site. The materials used are standard for a building dating from the second half of the 20th century: a concrete floor with little or no insulation, walls of metal sandwich panels insulated with 10cm of fibreglass and a slightly inclined roof of the same material with an asphalt covering.

According to our latest study, 69% of heat is lost through the roof, 11% through the walls (mainly due to the loading bays which are not equipped with double doors) and 11% through the ground. This last figure surprised me the most.

During the 2009-2010 financial year, we spent €35,000 on gas for heating only (1200mW, or 90,000m³ of gas) and €280,000 on nuclear-generated electricity (or 4.8gW) for the motors of the machines, the vacuum pumps, the sorting station for paper off-cuts, the ink mixer and lighting in the workshops and offices.

A real black hole! Financially as much as environmentally.

A first 'eco renovation' project took precedence and we planned it from various angles. We redesigned the insulation, step by step, in the roof, the walls, the openings onto the loading bays and the ground.

Our energy efficiency immediately went up because we lowered our expenditure on energy consumption. By replacing gas with geothermal energy, we completed the process and reduced the time taken to see a return on investment still more. All this without even mentioning the benefit to the environment and staff comfort in general.

By making these investments jointly, our environmental impact decreased significantly and our activity became more ecological and economical as regards energy.

Solutions which complement one another are helpful. Inspired by the functioning of any ecosystem, we chose to connect and coordinate rather than implementing individual solutions. Experience shows us that this is more efficient.

Getting to grips with consumption on the production line

This includes, for instance, the energy consumption of our machinery. How could we reduce it substantially? At the time, we dried our envelopes with blowers, which were very heavy users of energy: about a third of the company's annual consumption, in the region of €100,000. We changed the system and now use infrared drying technology, reducing our energy consumption by three-quarters to €25,000 a year. In one fell swoop, we benefitted the environment, saved money and improved working conditions because the old system, with blowers, used to give off a lot of heat in the summer.

Another priority was to change the vacuum pumps. In 2008, we made enquiries and discovered that the technology had made great steps forward in the last few years. We chose equipment with a screw system (rather than clutches), which meant pumping power could be adapted to demand.

These more controllable machines consume less energy and make less noise. It is an important consideration because the old machines exceeded 110 decibels and needed a specially insulated room, which was at odds with the need for fresh air for cooling. It meant we made too much noise, even off-site. The new, quieter machines can be enclosed in a new, insulated room in the middle of the factory. The hot air, which is inevitably produced when high or low pressure vacuum pumps compress air, is retained for heating the factory.

All this reorganisation meant we were able to stop and dismantle two of the four gas boilers (and, at the same time, get rid of the asbestos that lined the flue).

I choose these examples because they are very typical. In fact, we went right through the company and changed everything. Little by little, progressively, following a methodology whereby we asked ourselves, with each investment: how can we do better in the future than we did in the past? Our waste recycling, the production of the energy we consume, the quality of our raw materials, our processes... Finally, over five years, once this balanced methodology had been implemented everywhere, our company, which had been in great financial difficulty in 1997, began generating profits of between 5 and 10%. All the while continuing, of course, to reinvest the money made by the company back into the company.

Flowers on the roof

When my team and I were speaking about the dilapidated state of our old roof (which had been built in about 1848), we could not bring ourselves to replace it with an identical one. A manufacturing company needs to make productive investments rather than spend money on repairing an unproductive and inert roof. We had to find a way of making the roof profitable and flourishing!

Because we had to renovate certain parts of our roof, we chose to do so by planting the surfaces, as we had a year previously on our office building. A green roof insulates but, more especially, it protects the structure and provides insulation. It does this so well that it is said to last more than fifty years. This little miracle is due to nature's marvellous resources. Indeed, the plants capture light and heat. The heat at the point of impact on a roof reaches 80°C when the sun is at its strongest, in summer. This melts the asphalt, which cracks when it cools overnight. More generally, it wears out surfaces, whatever they may be... except plants. If we plant the roof, heat and sunlight provide the plants' energy (photosynthesis). Under the networks of foliage, micro-vortices of air ventilate, reducing and stabilising the temperature, in summer, at 25°C. The dust in the atmosphere settles on the leaves, which feed off it and which absorb water through the roots. This virtually complete ecosystem requires little maintenance.

We chose sedums, semi-succulents recommended by a regional botanical laboratory, which grow naturally in the crevices of walls. It would have been a mistake to import an invasive and non-endemic species.[1]

Being an industrial building, the roof slopes only slightly. But plants can also grip onto the steep roofs of private houses. There are anchoring systems which are very efficient up to 30°C or a 58% slope.[2]

Our green roof does not recreate the exact same permeability as its equivalent on the ground, but it makes a large contribution to reducing the impact of our building on its environment. Rainwater is captured by the root systems of the plants and retained in small containers on the roof; 50 to 60% of storm water can be saved this way. The majority of the liquid is then evapotranspired by the plant itself. If all roofs in urban areas were planted, the ambient temperature would go down naturally by up to two degrees over a few years, while the hygrometry rate would go up.[3]

To date, there is no man-made substance which can offer so many simple and efficient answers to roofing problems. This applies wherever you live. Only plants can adapt so well to climate, rainfall and temperature, but also to prevailing winds. There are roofs protected by plants as far north as Norway, across Germany, as well as in California.

Those who live or work under a green roof agree: the benefits are felt both in terms of sound and thermal insulation. We have noticed an

---

1. See *Green Roof Plants*, Edmund and Lucie Snodgrass, Timber Press, 2006.

2. See *Planting Green Roofs and Living Walls*, Nigel Dunnett and Noel Kingsbury, Timber Press, 2004, pp. 67-68.

3. See 'How cities can beat the heat', *Nature*, 26th August, 2015.
www.bit.ly/ecolonomy03

enormous difference in the offices at Pocheco. We have done away with all electric heating convectors and air conditioning diffusers. They have been replaced by underfloor gas heating fired by a condensing boiler.

The benefits of a green roof extend beyond rainwater management. For instance, roof plants form a safe microenvironment for many birds and pollinating insects.

The renovation work on our office roofs cost €250,000 for an area of 2,200m^2 (we replaced the whole roof and the frame was strengthened because it was not designed to take the weight of the plants). On the other hand, we calculate the resulting energy savings at €10,000 a year, meaning our investment would be repaid over twenty-five years at the most, since the building has other depreciation factors.

With this success under our belt, we chose to develop a plan for renovating our industrial building a year later. This was on another level entirely, because the building in question covers 8,000m^2 in all. The initial budget estimates reached €2 million, even if we only dealt with a quarter of the whole surface. However, as long as we could sustain a 20-year return on investment, and allowing for the operator's ability to change their buy-back rates for electricity, this project could finance and pay for itself in full.[4]

An architect's expertise is absolutely essential for a job like this. Renovating a factory roof entails obvious restrictions, such as not being able to stop production while the work is in progress!

Many directors of industrial companies would prefer to move and start afresh, even if it means building new premises, rather than grapple with a renovation. Today, I can confidently say that they are missing a trick. I can testify to the enormous interest of such a project for the company and for the team and I hope that the figures presented here will help them change their minds.

Among other benefits, this work has introduced us to technologies and suppliers that were previously unknown to us. It was a welcome

---

[4]. My figures do not include the grants we are entitled to for our various projects. Still, I owe it to the integrity of my story to specify that our supplier's buy-back rate for electricity is heavily subsidised by the French state. It should also be noted that new energy sources have always been subsidised by the state. Otherwise, the nuclear power programme would never have got off the ground. In my opinion, nothing makes this clearer than reading *La Vérité sur le nucléaire (The truth about nuclear power)*, Corinne Lepage, Éditions du Seuil, 2011.

enrichment. We chose to work with local small and medium-sized companies and we always met the foreman and manager. Direct and regular contact with the teams means promises and deadlines are kept and the inevitable surprises encountered on a worksite can be solved calmly and professionally. In contrast, preparations are drawn-out. I got a little impatient; I was wrong. It is an absolutely crucial phase in the success of such a job. If it was up to me, not one square metre of new or renovated roofing would be built in France today without being planted.

Sunshine

On the factory roof, we have installed 600m² of hybrid-technology solar panels which were manufactured and assembled in Germany.

As the name suggests, thermal solar energy means heat can be harnessed, especially the natural calories present in sunrays. In short, these thermal panels are made up of a pane of glass, a black surface which absorbs heat, an insulator to keep the heat in and, inside, a copper coil through which a heat transfer fluid flows and stores the calories. This source of heat can be used for domestic hot water, as with solar water heaters, or put into the heating system for greater output. Even so, an extra energy source, such as gas or electricity, is always required in order to bridge the gaps when there is no sunshine.

As for recyclability, the majority of solar panels contain recyclable components such as glass, plastic or aluminium. Even their silicon cells can be melted down to make new cells! In other words, this solution fitted perfectly with our objectives.

Geothermal

When the remaining two gas boilers came to the end of their days, we had to replace them, taking into account the fact that our investments had to respect our three criteria: making working conditions easier and/or safer, reducing the impact on the environment and reducing production costs.

The profitability calculations proved that the new geothermal system would cost the same to run as the old system of gas heating. This time, we had to bite the bullet and accept that the new system we were going to choose would not enable us to reduce financial costs.

Geothermal[5] energy needs electricity to feed the pumps which provide circulation in the system. Electricity, however, is four times the price of gas (as of August 2010).

Turning off the gas was a radical choice that I wished to implement, because this non-renewable resource generates major environmental costs (gas pipelines several thousand kilometres long, refineries, other forms of transport...), although I don't have an LCA to prove it.

There is one other matter to look at, that of nuclear-generated electricity. On the one hand, we reduced our consumption by insulating our premises better and, on the other hand, by re-using the heat produced by our envelope production process. We also know that it is profitable to produce photovoltaic electricity. Nevertheless, we consume more than 4 million kW per year and, with the gas equivalent, another million kW. In view of such a volume, our efforts to harness daylight for lighting seem derisory!

Wind power

As soon as we are financially able, we intend to buy a wind turbine to be situated 50km from the factory, on a special site, a wind farm in fact. The contraption will be perched 135m up, on an outcrop, itself over 170m high (which, in our flat region, is a mountain!), bigger than a juggernaut trailer and will produce 2,000kW/h depending on wind strength and regularity. The wind blows night and day and production is continuous. This power will be enough to cover (with a little left

---

5. Geothermal energy is the only really renewable energy catering for the production of heat and/or electricity. It functions on the following principle: pumps extract water from underground basins at a given point and depth. Depending on depth and geography, the temperature of this water varies from <30 °C to >250 °C. Once at the surface, the water runs through a specially-adapted network, gives off the difference in temperature, and is then fed back into the basin according to the direction the underground water flows in.

There are three uses for geothermal energy, depending on the temperature and depth of the water extracted: very low (<30°C ; <100m) for heating or air conditioning; low and medium (30°C - 100°C; 1,000m - 4,000m), used in urban or industrial heating networks; high (>250°C; 1,500m - 3,000m) for producing electricity with turbines. Very low-temperature geothermal energy can be put to use all over the world, unlike the other systems which are suitable only in very specific places. In 2002, the ratio of energy consumed to energy produced was as follows for heat networks: 1kW/h : 4kW/h.

over) our annual consumption (electricity and gas combined). Accordingly, we will be able to say that our envelopes are produced using wind power and that having, by these means, easily compensated for nuclear energy, we will have a factory running on passive energy.

In financial terms, a new, state-of-the-art windpower plant, like the one described here, costs €2 million. On top of this come charges for the connection, the meters and maintenance (which for a machine such as this costs more than €50,000 a year). In return for this, the contract with the operator is signed for a duration of between ten and fifteen years, depending on the quantity actually produced. They buy each kW/h for €0.082. Return on investment will be achieved in under ten years, or nearer six according to our latest estimate.

And water…

As soon as you build roads, car parks, buildings or airports you make the ground impermeable. Each drop of water trickles and you have to 'manage' this flow. Now, as everyone knows, it only rains twice a year in the north of France, once for six months and once for three months…

At Pocheco, as the renovation of our roof progresses, we bury tanks and collect rain water through pipes using a siphon system.[6] Thus, 80% of the water used in the factory is rain water. This goes on watering the plants (except those in the bamboo plantation) and is used for the toilets: a site working 24 hours a day with 104 people equals three hundred cisterns of water a day, or 300m^3 a year. If there is any left over, we save it in a tank for the driest months. If there is still more left over, we pour it onto the bamboo. We also intend to put possible surplus water at the disposal of our neighbours, who are individual homeowners and not all equipped with tanks. Water is a major question for many around the world and it has become a real energy issue. Let's not waste it!

---

6. The siphon system for collecting rain water from roofs is 'low pressure', the opposite of 'gravitational'. It stops air entering the pipes and increases the flow of water. As a result, the pipes are three times smaller and deposits are flushed out by water pressure, as well as being filtered at the point of collection.

Energy Management at Pocheco

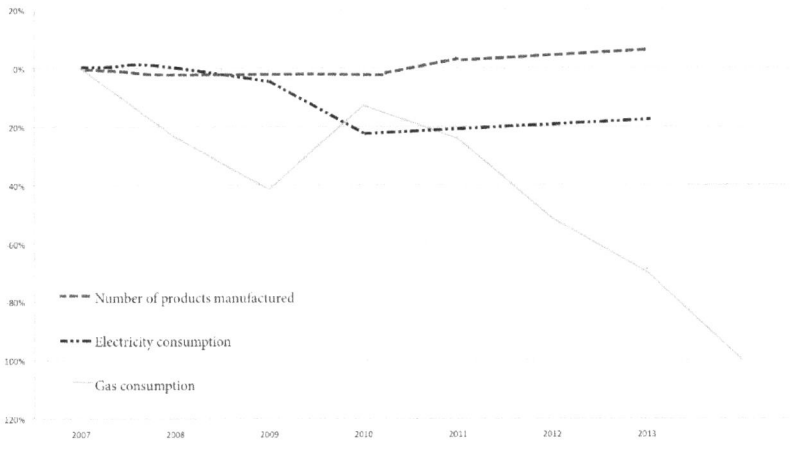

Number of products manufactured compared to energy consumption

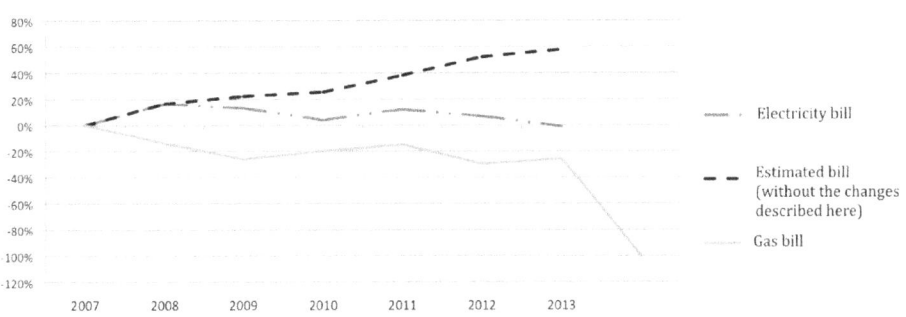

Energy bills (electricity and gas)

Energy: POCHECO Key Figures

Economical	Ecological
€150,000 / year energy savings	€360,000 kg CO₂e/year saved
€85,000 / year energy production	

Eco*lo*nomy

Water Management at Pocheco

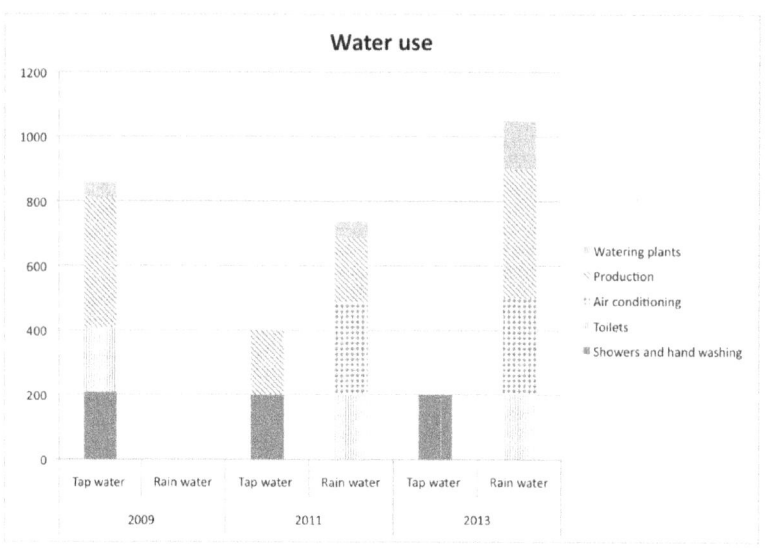

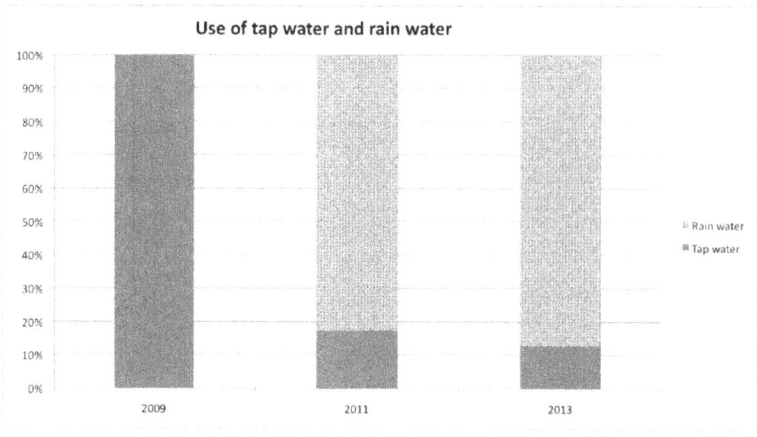

Water: POCHECO Key Figures

Economical	Ecological
Reduction by 77% in use of tap water	100m³ rainwater storage capacity
€5,500/year tap water savings	

Biodiversity at Pocheco

Timeline for reintegration of biodiversity on our production site

2009	April	Planting of green roof (office) (200m²).
2011	March	Planting green roof (factory) (1200m²).
	April	Installation of 4 beehives.
	May	Installation of bamboo plantation.
2012	April	Installation of 4 beehives.
	May	More green roof (100m²).
2013	July	Emergency access vegetalised (1280 m²).
	August	Installation of bird and bat nests.
2014	January	Opening of garden « 11 rue des Roloirs » (400m²).
	February	Partnership with two local farmers for our « Paniers de Marianne » fruit and veg boxes.
		Planting 280m hedges.
	March	Planting conservation (and 'scrumping') orchard (800m²).
	April	Plantation of 300 raspberry bushes.
		More bamboo.
	May	Green roof installed on the new warehouse and maintenance workshop and AGORA workshop (1,120 m²).
	July	Vegetalisation of the new water storage tank.
	October/November	Inauguration of POCHECO as an officially recognised bird shelter.

Eco*lo*nomy

BIODIVERSITY AT POCHECO
A map of our production site

Chapter 8

Our waste is a treasure!

Optimising waste is a new idea in industry. For a long time, we have been happy to get rid of waste, and to do as as cheaply as possible. The idea of upgrading it came from the realisation that, with imagination and will, a company can convert its waste into a real resource. Indeed, many materials considered to be waste can be reused in different ways: either by recycling the actual product and making it into something else which is then put back into circulation, or by using it to produce energy.

At Pocheco, we are convinced that all waste can and must be processed and that all ideas for optimising it are good. At first, I didn't think we would manage. As we looked into it, we found waste in ever-increasing abundance! How on earth did we manage to produce such quantity and variety? There was waste from our manufacturing and our renovation, but also from our dirty water and even our air.

Inks, glue and paper

By going back to basics and capitalising on the knowledge of our suppliers, we have, little by little, been able to select components more wisely, reduce their quantity and variety and look for larger consignments.

Take the example of inks. As described earlier, we decided to make certain mixtures in-house. A mixer means we can use 200-litre containers of primary colours and are able to blend the quantity of ink required to the nearest decilitre. The leftovers are mixed and produce a very useful background grey.

Recycling water

At Pocheco, as in any industry where paper plays a rôle, the water used must be treated as waste. Naturally, we gave thought to how this water could be put to good use and we found a solution, namely 'phytoremediation', a somewhat clumsy word referring to the technique of collecting dirty water and using the chemistry of plants to clean it. Indeed, certain plants have root systems which are able to break down the polluting molecules and use them as nutriments.

Until recently, a specialist company used to come and collect our process water once a month. The environmental cost of this was a lorry travelling 2,400km a year to transport dirty water. In other words: 3,060kg CO_2e. The financial cost of this collection was €20,000 a year. If you listen to the water board experts, what they say leaves little doubt: the nearer a raindrop falls to the place it is to be treated before going back into the ground, the better it is for everyone.

Now, it's possible to reduce our general impact on the environment, and in particular that of our dirty water, by creating bamboo plantations in our towns and near our factories and office blocks. Bamboo is a giant grass. People talk of bamboo prairies and over 1,500 species are listed around the world. It adapts to all climates and its propagation by invasive rhizomes is easily limited with geotextiles.

Bamboo is a general-purpose plant, in the best sense of the term. It is more resistant than oak or metal, or even kevlar. Scaffolding is made of bamboo all over Asia... Try to snap a bamboo twig: it bends but can only be broken with the greatest difficulty.

It can also be used as fuel for domestic heating because it generates three times more heat than our usual firewood. The LHV[1] of bamboo is 4,500, higher than oak (4,300) and only slightly lower than coal (4,700).

At the end of its life cycle (in our part of the world, the plant's filtering capacity diminishes after four years), bamboo is cut down and dried, after which the biomass, transformed into granules, is used as fuel. So it's a natural product which, unlike its competitors, doesn't shed its leaves in winter (it continues working) and doesn't produce the sewage sludge which is so complicated to get rid of.

Bamboo is efficient as soon as it is planted. Its root system develops very quickly, activates bacteria and does its job of filtering and breaking down molecules. It can be used for soil remediation (even in the case of heavy metals, hydrocarbons or nuclides) by feeding on effluents laden with dirty liquids, releasing oxygen into the air and capturing CO_2.

---

1. Lower Heating Value or, put simply, the heating power of materials.

Finally, a bamboo bed also provides an excellent natural fire screen because its fibre is saturated with water. Birds nest in this natural barrier where biodiversity can develop. The whole natural environment is altered. So is the economic environment, because a new sector for maintaining bamboo beds and processing the wood produced could very well emerge.

Of course, we felt we had to try this experiment in phytoremediation. Our factory is ideally situated in the heart of a village surrounded by fields and a magnificent urban park – an exceptional site in our region which is sorely lacking in woodland.[2] We occupy 13,000m², of which 8,000 are built on. At the beginning, a large area of the site was left under grass. Then tarmac took over more or less everything. As our renovations have progressed, we have chosen to reverse the trend and reduce impermeable zones.

A bamboo bed with complete drainage system installed by specialist engineers costs €280,000 (the couple who invented it[3] are as straightforward and efficient as their idea). The cost of our investment will be recouped in under six years.

The only disadvantage of phytoremediation is the amount of ground space which has to be turned over to nature. Depending on the type of pollution and the volumes of water in question, this can quickly reach several thousand square metres.

We have put our natural 'purification plant', which is odourless and without lagoon systems, at the entrance to our premises. It is an ideal place for people to arrive and be welcomed and is landscaped and eco-efficient. And nothing is wasted any longer.

With the benefit of experience, I can say that not one more square metre should be built on in France without provision in the immediate vicinity of the building for a space serving to collect and purify water.

---

2. We have woodland cover of only 7%, compared with 27% for the country as a whole. The vice-president of the regional council, Emmanuel Cau, has introduced an ambitious reforestation plan and Pocheco has set up a non-profit reforestation association to support the regional programme.

3. Véronique Arfi and Bernard Benayoun of Phytorem. You should hear them and their team talking about the qualities of bamboo for the natural sanitisation of all our effluents, to understand the economic and ecological absurdity of oversized purification plants. They have installed bamboo beds as far away as Mauritius. I owe the information I set out here to them and their ten years of research, supported by the CNRS.

Circularity and its advantages

On the subject of waste, the heart of the village where our factory is situated is due to undergo extensive rebuilding. A social housing development will soon be replacing a disused factory. The site can be depolluted by planting bamboo on it. Bamboo's purifying function can be activated by filtering dirty water from the village through it. And rather than adding new capacity to the local sewage works, why not plant out a field left fallow with bamboo? The farmer would keep his job and would also learn a new one: farmer-depolluter. Finally, a new job is created for someone to come and live on the new development, learn how to take care of the bamboo field and make heating pellets.

The village wants to reduce the heating costs of the school and the new retirement home, both of which are in the process of being built. They have chosen a passive-energy system with an additional central boiler, to be fuelled by bamboo pellets. Starting with waste, circularity can be set up. The village develops its capacities and preserves its green belt, which produces collective assets.

In this circular organisation, which begins with recycling water, bamboo is useful for purifying, employment, industrial activity, reducing building on green belt areas and means less traffic travelling between home and work.

Maybe you think that all this is unrealistic. But our experience shows that this approach can be adapted to any situation.

Recycling air

Our manufacturing processes do not require a finely controlled air temperature. To cool the air in summer, we opted for a very simple recycling technique which has no impact on the environment – unlike air conditioning systems which use energy and gases that pollute the atmosphere if released into the air at the end of their life cycle.

This system, termed adiabatic, simply involves capturing air higher up in the building, directing it towards a filter, which resembles the chambers in a honeycomb, made up of cellulose fibres (cardboard, of sorts) and very abundantly sprayed with water – the run-off water from our roof that we save in a tank does an excellent job.

The result: air cooled by three or four degrees is sent back into the workshop and improves everyone's comfort a great deal.

Roofs create waste

But that's not all. I asked the team to think about how we could reuse the waste that was collected when we took down our 2,200m² of saw-tooth roofing (a roof in the shape of saw teeth with one glazed side, typical of industrial buildings). This waste was mainly made up of the wooden frame, wattle and daub, glass, zinc and roof tiles. In fact, it is moving to think that these materials resisted bad weather and insects for a hundred and fifty years, with no treatment. Wood hardens with time. We will reuse it for an office floor or insulating cladding for outside. Meanwhile, we have removed all the nails and soaked it all in flax oil. This perfectly natural treatment allows regional woods to be used and protected for many years to come.

A local horticulturalist came to collect the tiles to grind them into dust. Mixed with a substrate, they will become compost for green fences or for the plants on our roof. The zinc was taken away by a scrap dealer who recycled it. All we threw out (after sorting) was the wattle and daub and the nails. That is also what eco*lo*nomy is all about! Less transport, less waste and less expense. As well as the satisfaction of seeing our old roof frame take on a new lease of life. And the pleasure of giving work to a local joiner.

Waste Management at Pocheco

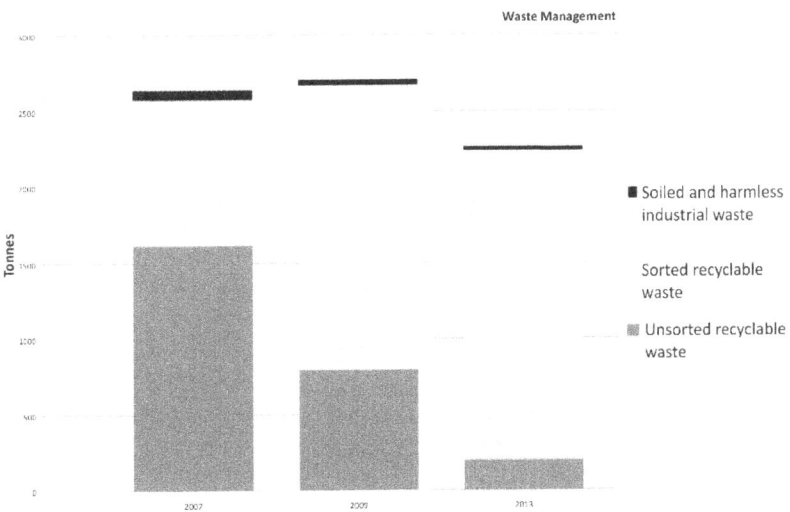

Waste: POCHECO Key Figures

Economical:	Ecological:
99% of our waste is recyclable 91% of our waste is sorted €360,000 /year savings	470,000 kg CO_2e / year savings

Eco*lo*nomies: POCHECO Key Figures

Actions		Investment	Annual cost	Annual eco*lo*nomies	Annual environmental savings (expressed in kg CO_2e)
Raw materials	Eco-design	€1,737,000	€62,000	€338,500	1,152,304
Organisation	Certifications		€20,000	€50,000	
Transport	Management			€27,000	122,000
Waste	On-site management	€180,000	€5,000	€360,000	470,000
Working conditions	Improvement	€702,187			
Water	Rainwater recovery	€103,000	€500	€5,500	425
Energy	Local production	€3,264,157	€23,860	€235,000	360,000
	Maximisation				
Noise	Renovation and diminution	€60,378			
Biodiversity	LPO, Associations, Green roof	€614,712		€15,000	
TOTAL		€6,661,434	€111,360	€1,031,000	2,104,729

And to summarise …

Reduction in Greenhouse gas emissions, 1996-2013:	Global return on investment	Total eco*lo*nomies since 1996
22%	7 years	€9,522,316

PART THREE

Finding Pleasure in Working as a Team

'If you get caught standing on your desk, you can say it was my fault!'

One day, an image came to me as I was waking from a nap under the centuries-old tropical trees in the botanical gardens of Lisbon.

I was lying on a bench and their foliage was protecting me from the hot mid-summer sunshine. Looking at the canopy above me, I noticed that the branches of each tree brushed against one another without overlapping, and so covering the widest area without losing contact with the direct sunlight.

I'm not a botanist, to my great regret. But I've read Francis Hallé and recommend him. He and his team of researchers invented the 'canopy raft' which enables them to carry out fruitful research above the canopy, the highest part of the tropical and equatorial forests and, by extension, the upper part of the trees' branches which are in contact with the sunlight.

I remembered the illustrations and the photo inside the cover of his book.[1] In it, he demonstrates that the canopy is an ecosystem which self-organises perfectly. Everything is linked to the whole in a balanced connection.

There's nothing to stop us taking inspiration from what already exists. I think a company can develop along these lines.

---

1. *Plaidoyer pour l'arbre,* Francis Hallé, Éditions Actes Sud, 2005.

Chapter 9

Giving the company a future

Diversification became an important question the day our firm was split off from the group it previously belonged to. And in order to plan this diversification of activities, we began by capitalising on the variety of people we have in our team, our wealth of experiences, backgrounds and cultures. We've learnt that when we listen to the point of view of a colleague whose experience is very different from our own, once the surprise has passed, we very quickly discover new options, new ideas. We work in creative pairs made up of very different people who enjoy working together. For instance, I work in a pair with my second in command, the production and purchasing manager. We're very complementary, having worked together for twenty years and often having different points of view! Our account managers all work in pairs too, which is also useful if ever one of them is away.

Faced with each other's different kinds of originality and creativity, these people have to formulate their thoughts in ever-clearer ways, which helps them find new directions and possibilities. This is the driving force behind our thinking on Pocheco's future.

The importance of research and checks

In Pocheco, change is a perfectly natural process, which often only needs to be steered and supported, no more. It avoids focusing on catching up with competitors because continuous improvement quickly makes copying obsolete. Even small firms can and should do R&D. And have ideas. What could be more accessible than an idea? Thought is available all the time and cannot be quantified in terms of cost. While an idea remains at the thought stage and is put up for consideration by the team, it costs very little. Time and intelligence – I truly believe that these wonderful driving forces of creative thought should be nurtured and used.

When you send out 100,000 statements a day, for example, you open 50 boxes of 2,000 envelopes. Multiplied by 210 working days a year, this makes 10,500 boxes. These then have to be flattened, stocked and recycled. Workers spend a lot of time doing these tasks and can develop musculo-skeletal illnesses. Indeed, a box of 2,000 envelopes weighs 10kg: 50 boxes a day equal 500kg, multiplied by 210 days makes 105 tonnes per year!

There is, however, an innovative packaging solution which consists of wrapping the envelopes around a reel with a winding-on machine, then unrolling them at the customer's site with an unwinding machine. This innovation requires no other handling than transporting the reels on a machine equipped with a special arm.

I asked a representative working with this system to come and show it to us. I found out that he did not know we existed. He had just spent two years going round all the European manufacturers and none of them had chosen to invest in the technology.

Nowadays, a third of our production volumes are packaged using this process. We have even become agents for the technology. We offer it for hire and there are only two of us, in Europe, promoting this reliable packaging method.

I am often surprised how our ideas flow. They stimulate us to have even more ideas and offer another benefit: it's difficult to copy us. This being so, I believe our creativity offers us more protection from our competitors than expensive patents which are often impossible to safeguard. And I don't believe that defences can be held long if you don't have a sure ability to move forward in the first place.

We do file patents, of course. With great pride, in fact. But the key is to look for innovative solutions. If we give ourselves the means, we can all become industrial innovators.

You don't need to be rich to develop solutions. It's quite enough to think, be very thorough and have a bit of imagination. Another example is quality control. In an ecosystem, all relations and interactions tend towards efficiency. In a company, quality control systems play a very important part in this. They are development processes like any other. They evolve, and so do norms. With time and a continuous simplification of procedures, the Pocheco team has transformed a complicated system into efficient solutions. The procedures, which meet Quality, Safety and Environmental standards, were written by the operators themselves. Then they were discussed and approved by our management and the certifying body we chose. They are still evolving.

Our procedures have allowed us to cut out all repetitive tasks and all intermediate levels in the hierarchy. Indeed, with this structure, each of us is answerable for the commitments we make. Who knows better than the machine operator how best to limit risk, reduce waste and increase efficiency and productivity? A system of random checks completes the procedure. In this way, we are constantly reducing our financial and environmental costs.

Diversifying our activities

One logical way to branch out is by diversifying our main activity into new services. For instance, given that we produce transactional envelopes, but that people often speak of the advantages of sending mail electronically, we are able to offer a system of 'hybrid' mail, bringing together the benefits of both. Our offer to customers is to install software for them which allows their staff to send their mail to an industrial printing centre where it is printed, inserted into envelopes and sent out. It is no longer necessary for them to print letters on their computers, put them in envelopes, frank them and post them. This enables the company to save on mail processing and, moreover, to reduce its carbon footprint.

Another route to diversifying our activity originated, not from our main activity but from the eco*lo*nomic renovation of our industrial premises. Since everything we have undertaken seems to work for us, and because we have gained considerable expertise in these matters, we offer to help other manufacturing companies along the same path. After all, we can be confident in recommending approaches we ourselves have put into practice: especially the choice of materials and construction techniques.

Constantly searching for organisational improvements and ways of diversifying which guarantee continuity of service for our co-workers and customers, we have built up a real wealth of good practice. So we went about setting up Pocheco Canopée Conseil, a consultancy in industrial eco*lo*nomy which accompanies firms in their search for eco*lo*nomies by proposing our solutions, all tested *in vivo*. A new procedure or technical change is only registered if it answers a real need, if it has no harmful effects on the person implementing or using it and, finally, if its impact on the environment is lower than that of the procedure it is replacing. These strict criteria are the essential condition for eco*lo*nomies to bring about gains in productivity.

For instance, after putting it into practice ourselves, we decided to include in Pocheco Canopée Conseil's service offer the LCA, life cycle assessment, meaning the precise scientific analysis of the impact of a given production on its environment (see Chapter 6).

Furthermore, each time we develop a new skill, we try to pass on the benefit of our research to other companies. This is how, over more than two years, we have developed several teams: one for industrial consulting, one for the reforestation of the Nord-Pas de Calais region, one for the development of 21st-century eco*lo*nomical techniques, one for the management of presorting and hybrid mail and yet another for the promotion of the 'green invoice' – an envelope carrying a bill or statement and informing customers of the ecological gesture that receiving paper mail represents.

We have not lost sight of the main fact: our trade is manufacturing envelopes. But we have acquired new expertise which assures the good health and continued existence of our company, in an industrial sector that has never been so precarious.

Eco*lo*nomy Valley

To provide a future for Pocheco, we have started new projects based on the principles of eco*lo*nomy. Today, we have the dream that the Nord-Pas de Calais region, on the strength of its 600 innovating ecocompanies, will be recognised as the spearhead of this new economy. Like California and its Silicon Valley, the Nord-Pas de Calais could be home to an Eco*lo*nomy Valley.

It would bring together innovative companies, run on the three founding principles of eco*lo*nomy which allow for business to develop locally, thereby creating a model that can be reproduced, gathering experience and feedback so as to spread good practice. Change the world? We could make a start today... In fact many citizens and other companies have already begun to concern themselves with the environment and living better (without waiting for me to write this book!).

Chapter 10

Eco*lo*nomy Valley begins with us

Update: it's July 2014 and I am returning to this text to revise it and bring it up to date. Looking back over the last two or three years, I realise that our efforts have drawn other manufacturers and district councils into the virtuous circle of eco*lo*nomy. The team at our research office, Pocheco Canopée Conseil, meet many people, including town councils and councillors; private companies, SMEs and larger businesses; business leaders and CSR managers. Almost all of them are interested in eco*lo*nomy, although some of them admit that it's not easy making it a priority. In most cases, they have no doubt about the tangible and measurable results presented by the team – the facts are clear and show that, for Pocheco and others, eco*lo*nomy works – but they have not yet managed to apply it in their own context.

How can we help them?

The work of time

You have to give yourself time. No procedure can be reformed by waving a magic wand. First of all, you need a close-knit team determined to change things.

The example of an SME in this region comes to mind. The manager came to see us after a conference. He was determined and had mobilised his team, who also showed sincere interest. We devised a first project together, to create a new product to widen his manufacturing range and test the commercial reaction – would customers go with the change? The manager and his team thought it would be a good way of taking a first collective step towards eco*lo*nomy. So we developed the new product. We suggested changing its structure. Part of it was made of polyester, which is petrochemical-based and difficult to recycle after use in an industrial process. As a replacement, we found a linen resin. The very heart of the product was altered: instead of being chemically based, it became organic and, hence, perfectly biodegradable. It was a step forward.

We carried out a full LCA on the updated product. We demonstrated that, on an industrial scale, production costs would be lower for the new version.

Then, silence. No more contact. Had they given up on the project? The question went unanswered.

After an experience like that, with the manager and his team pulling out, I sometimes think that the outlook is bleak. At Pocheco, we have taken nearly twenty years to steer our structures and ways of working towards eco*lo*nomy. It may seem a long time, but our experience here can help companies speed up their own revolution.

For district councils, the question is rather different, but may also lead to failure, due to their very long decision-making processes. They are obliged by law to implement complex selection cycles, sometimes resulting in situations which are difficult to explain to the team.

For instance, we met a local official who had begun renovation works in part of the town under his responsibility. Several meetings took place and seemed to be really very productive. He understood us, found our arguments relevant, encouraged us and gave us advice. We made steady progress together. The project plan was drawn up and ready to be put into action. It was exciting.

Then there was silence. A few days passed, a week, then two. We managed to get through to the official, who had suddenly become impossible to find or contact. He said that the job had to be put out to tender.

Make no mistake: I am in no way opposed to competition – I always find it stimulating and I never expect to jump the queue. But we had produced our best ideas without the official telling us the rules clearly. He had told us that eco*lo*nomy 'could not be opened up to competition' because we alone knew how to implement it and 'our project would take a different legal route'. We thought we were the only ones on the job. Nevertheless, at odds with what the official had said, a call for tender was issued. We were not selected and all our preparatory work was passed on to the company that bid against us. Enough said.

Luckily, other councils see their plans through and Pocheco does not depend on its eco*lo*nomy consultancy to make a living!

Optimistic or naïve?

Some people think we must be complete novices for acting so naïvely. But do we need to wrap ourselves in legal protection every time we put an idea forward? Do we really need to reach the critical mass of the large international consultancy firms in order to see through changes in the company without being swindled? Well, we chose to persevere. The team and I decided to carry on tirelessly offering our services, without our survival depending on the profitability of our design office, allowing our proposals to take root in the minds of our potential customers.

Are we any less eager for achievement? What about our impatience and the ideas we have not yet put into practice?

We have decided to apply the ideas we have invented for others to ourselves. So that the many visitors who come to our site, not all of whom are decision-makers, can draw from what we have done and find the resources for their own personal revolutions. And perhaps one day, when they themselves are decision-makers, they will be in a position to influence the transition.

Until that time, or at least until a healthy number of our clients have succeeded in their ecolonomical projects, we are continuing our little domestic revolution. The following pages explain how it bears fruit daily in our company and in others.

The Ecolonomy Village

Instead of founding an Ecolonomy Valley here and now, as I had hoped when the first French edition of this book was published, we decided to found an Ecolonomy Village, on the company's premises, which we have expanded through the recent purchase of two small houses with gardens adjoining our factory.

Following a wide-ranging discussion with my colleagues Élodie, Kevin and Maxime, the house at number 11, rue de Roloirs, will be called *le Fol Espoir*. On the ground floor is a large area, which will be renovated and opened to the public and, with the team from the not-for-profit Maison de l'*écol*onomie (Ecolonomy Centre), become a 'repair café' managed by Samy and Gary's team. People will be able to bring their mechanical or electronic devices for repair and a 'de-obsolescence' programme, while they enjoy the soup of the day, a sandwich or a drink. You can have your household appliances repaired so that they last longer than the four or five years programmed by the makers. Raw materials are rare and should be preserved! These repairs will be carried out by a team of technicians at Pocheco. After all, we are seasoned technicians. We train young apprentices in our maintenance workshop, which is equipped with the most high-performance technology (grinding, digital lathes and milling machines). Expertise in mechanics, electricity and all sorts of automatic devices, sharing and passing on knowledge – these are inexhaustible resources.

At *le Fol Espoir*, we will also house a collective ecological laundry service, as not everyone may want to own their own washing machine: you fill a bag and drop it off when you arrive for work, then you pick up your clean washing at the end of the day. Collective washing in large-capacity machines, themselves powered by electricity produced on our roof, using rainwater heated by panels and their solar water heater, ecological detergent and our waste water filtered by our bamboo plants… it all makes for closed-loop self-sufficiency. Our local resources (water and energy) are sufficient for us to deal with large quantities of washing, thereby reducing household consumption of energy and water by customers, colleagues and/or neighbours who belong to our Eco*lo*nomy Centre.

In an annexe on the ground floor of *le Fol Espoir*, our colleagues sell fruit and vegetables grown by farmers in our village and a village nearby. Local, seasonal and weekly fruit and veg boxes – which we have christened *Paniers de Marianne* – came into being. Maxime and Mélissa serve our customers and manage operations with Rémy and Hugues, our producers.

We are lucky to work in a semi-rural locality, because agriculture is still very present here. The fields are not big enough for enormous machinery to operate, which is also lucky. There is no intensive agriculture here, with its array of pesticides. Small quantities are grown, enriching the soil season after season, and allowing the farmers to make a living from their work – because these farmers receive no subsidies (they go mainly to large farms). As citizens, often living near these little farms, we can show solidarity and, as well as feeding our families with healthy produce, help farmers out of poverty and provide them with work.

Additionally, there are no middlemen: 80% of the price of a veg box goes to its producer, 20% covers the admin., sales and marketing.

Obviously, the purpose of our organisation is not to make a profit, but everyone has to be paid for their work.

Our fruit and veg boxes have been so successful that we've joined up with a distributor of organic and fair-trade produce to open our 'Marianne's market'. It's in the annexe and open every day. It's a collection point for fresh produce, fruit and vegetables, and our neighbours no longer need to take the car out to get supplies during the week.

The main room in *le Fol Espoir* is given over to our 'repair café'. In the summer, the room opens out onto the garden. We are very keen to develop these activities.

On the first floor of *le Fol Espoir*, there are rooms fitted out for Pilates, yoga or BodyPump (particularly popular on the coldest winter days), or for muscle toning classes or appointments with our osteopath. Showers and changing rooms complete the offer. Our qualified instructors train and guide us in running and Nordic walking. Naturally, these lessons are open to our neighbours and to visitors to the village – everything is covered by membership of our Ecolonomy Centre.

On the second and top floor of *le Fol Espoir*, new offices will house the Canopée Conseil R&D team. All the planning and architectural design for renovating *le Fol Espoir*, from the initial idea, through the scheduling, choice of materials, phasing of the work, design of the structure and the finished appearance of the project – from applying for the building permit to the choice of craftsmen – everything was devised, discussed, chosen and imagined by the same team. Each new step is something new for them to learn, then the steps can be repeated for other programmes we might work on.

The Ecolonomy Centre idea is due to be replicated in four local towns and we aim to develop our activities and spread our ideas as far as possible. If people are happy with what our Ecolonomy Centres offer, then we can hope that they will soon spread around the country and, who knows, even further afield.

An ecolonomic renovation

Before it became *le Fol Espoir*, No. 11, rue des Roloirs was a normal house. It was probably built with the factory, in around 1848, to house the owner's family. We kept to our experimental method and chose to re-use the materials that we dismantled. The roof tiles were transformed into clay pellets and became the new substrate for the planted section of the new roof. The wood from the old roof frame was too damaged and fragile to support the new structure, so we turned it into wooden flooring. The advantage of re-using such 150-year-old material is that insects do not burrow into wood which has hardened over time. We didn't have to use one drop of varnish or insecticide on our new floor. No VOCs on the one hand, no waste on the other. The old aluminium frames were given to an organisation which distributes them to individuals. The windows didn't meet our needs and the panes of glass were also re-used.

We chose under-floor heating for the ground floor and our calculations showed that the average temperature throughout the house would be between 19 and 20°C. In the sports rooms and office, additional heating is provided by wood-burning stoves.

Three technologies are combined on the roof: photovoltaic panels for lighting in the house; solar water heating panels for the showers, kitchen, under-floor heating and the ecological laundry; plants covering any free space on the roof enable rain water to be collected and redistributed for users' needs.

Thanks to the insulating qualities of today's windows, we have considerably increased the glazed surfaces, bringing in daylight wherever possible without bothering our neighbours. To insulate the roof space adequately, we chose certified glueless wood wool, which contains no VOCs. As for renovating the floors, a good sanding did the job.

All in all, the renovation was eco*lo*nomical on many levels, but I would stress the fact that, by renovating an existing site, we did not add to the loss of greenfield land, a major problem for our society, which continues to dogmatically promote growth as the only option. If we don't want to be forced to downsize in a few years' time, we must start now by renovating whenever possible, rather than covering more land.

Recycling and salvage

We undertook something similar when we rebuilt an old workshop in the yard. Over time it had become a sort of junk room and the roof was about to cave in. Our research office took complete charge of the rebuild (we called the project Agora). It was a rebuild, rather than a renovation, because we only kept the walls of the old building.

The 19th-century tile roof became a green roof with a substrate of clay pellets made from the crushed tiles.

We are now used to collecting water and local plants, so that, in five years, our green roofs have come to represent practically 50% of the surface covered by our buildings. Our premises are 220m^2 in area and reach almost 5 metres at their apex, which leaves a lot of room inside. At ground level is a coil heating system, connected to our wood-burning central boiler, and a recycled concrete slab.

Recycled concrete? Once again, you only have to ask. We build a lot in France, but we also demolish. Rather than overloading our tips with concrete rubble or dredging the ocean beds to satisfy our greed for coarse sand to make concrete, it's possible, even desirable, to ask your builder to use salvaged or recycled materials. A project in progress can often be synchronised with another one nearby, with a corresponding reduction in the impact of transporting the building materials. The demolition site supplies the materials your builder needs for your renovations and recycling is quick and easy.

The same applies to asphalt. Our new lorry yard is perfectly suitable for the regular flow of juggernauts. Nonetheless, it is entirely surfaced with salvaged asphalt. Why encourage the production of asphalt rather than recycling it?

To return to Agora, it has become a new workshop. It has been planned as a multi-purpose room designed to accommodate up to 150 people. Like cats, our buildings have several lives.

The adjacent yard still needs redesigning. Once we have the money, we will remove its asphalt surface, expose the earth and plant wild flowers and a lime tree, because our bee colonies are also growing. We started with four hives which soon grew to twelve and, now, we have twenty-four hives on our site, with a production capacity of 300 kilos of honey per year.

You are the future of eco*lo*nomy!

While we wait for an Eco*lo*nomy Valley, whose good practices would spread little by little to the whole region and even further afield, boosting business without destroying extra resources, we have made a start on creating an Eco*lo*nomy Village. You have to start somewhere! Our dream is that this village will be the inspiration for others. Even so, when I see the coaches dropping off our visitors from all over the world, I sometimes fear that our village, like the famous little Gaulish village in the Asterix cartoon, will become an isolated spectacle rather than eco*lo*nomy being taken up and used everywhere as a contemporary method of development.

What happens to our Eco*lo*nomy Village obviously depends on us, the team, but it also clearly depends on what our readers and visitors decide. They will either expand our experiment and come to strengthen our community, or they will deem it to be the public authorities' business and place their trust in the vagaries of decisions which, all too often, lead to poor and inefficient results.

Eco*lo*nomy is a recipe for hard times. We have to be clear: public finances are over-stretched and rather than dealing with the problem by reducing social security cover even further, we have to consider changing our way of thinking. No more 'growth at any price' – a concept which is clearly unsustainable now – but full-on eco*lo*nomy! Companies will adapt to this new way of working, there is no doubt about that. Our experience must be the first of very many.

As I write this, we are working on convincing a number of giant companies to cover their millions of square metres of roofing with plants, so as to capture rain water and cool the air – instead of using unhealthy, energy-guzzling air conditioning – or with solar panels. What we offer on the scale of a factory and its site is perfectly applicable to others. It's a question of conviction and choice. It's much easier to set the ball rolling than people think.

People I speak to often wonder how they can start an eco*lo*nomy programme. Obviously, our answer depends on each individual situation. But in each case, we begin with action. Lao-tzu wrote that the longest journeys always begin with a first step.

In other words, *le Fol Espoir*, its myriad activities, and the Agora, with its wealth of diversification for our industrial activities, are our case studies – our references for passing knowledge on, along with the learning and development areas in our talent pool.

These are the most recent testimonies to our efforts for a transition towards a more local economy, more respectful of natural resources, thriftier, but no less productive or profitable, quite the opposite! Eco*lo*nomy helps build a reassuring future.

Chapter 11

The company, a pool of talent and activities

We have always believed in our project and it has worked! We believe that a successful corporate-citizen plan should be based on diversity. Bringing together, on one industrial site, technicians and researchers, artists and inventors from different cultures – professionals whose backgrounds, expertise and plans would never normally have led them to meet and speak to one another. Except here, with a coffee at the café in our Eco*lo*nomy Centre, or during an outing to plant hedgerows or take care of farmland trees with the team from our reforestation organisation.[1]

Why not try reindustrialisation?

We have heard so much defeatist talk about deindustrialisation which, in the north of France, has had drastic consequences among the 230,000 workers in the area, as well as on the unemployment rate (still around 14%), that we are well-placed to find solutions, even seemingly original ones.

And why not? Why not consider reindustrialisation, 21st-century style? At Pocheco, the systems and standards we have implemented allow our employees to make the decisions, because the money earnt by the company is all reinvested back into the company, thereby becoming a means to an end. Through regular training and by working in small groups, the talents of my team are revealed. They get the confidence to make decisions and take risks. I don't believe that my team leave their brains in their lockers when they start work. Adjusting fast, powerful, unpredictable and demanding industrial machinery

---

1. Pocheco Canopée Reforestation: non-profit organisation: www.pochecocanopeereforestation.org

takes a level head and a great deal of expertise and intelligence. And dealing with these fragile mechanisms takes hands and a brain that need training.

At Pocheco, the mission of our managers is to pool and promote the potential of our teams.

The factory is located in the village of Forest-sur-Marque. A few years ago, we had a debate with members of the local council. The question was whether to keep our factory in the heart of the village, which has tended heavily towards residential development, or to move the company to an industrial estate.

The council maintained that if companies left the villages, then these villages would become little more than dormitories with, as a consequence, increased traffic and less vibrancy. They, therefore, suggested we stay in the village but move to a site on the outskirts.

We thought about it for several months. The economic and ecological costs of a new building, along with the fact that the plot was not well suited to being developed, were serious sticking points. But what finally helped us make up our minds was quite different.

Our industrial site, as old as it was, suited our needs. The buildings were dilapidated, the roof was leaking here and there, some areas were hardly used, but our walls represented our past all the same. Our factory was laden with meaning. Both practically and emotionally, it was irreplaceable. Moreover, it was going to be cheaper to renovate than to build something new.

All this has since turned out to be true, economically and ecologically.

I believe the meaning we attach to the quality of our products, our training programmes and our maintenance is what distinguishes our products from those of our competitors and that our factory plays a large part in this meaning.

We speak about the character of a private house or a notable site. Our factory has its character – its soul – too. Our factory site is 13,000m^2 and is situated between an urban nature reserve, a farm, a primary school and a development of detached houses, many of which were built by the site's first owner.

The site is well-integrated into the village. It is a benefit and a focal point for many professionals, without whom the village would never have been put on the map!

A talent pool

The different members of my team have arrived at Pocheco in the most unlikely ways.

Tao was only twenty when this book was being written. We met at the end of an environmental conference in Lille, in 2010. He was nearing the end of his graduate studies at a business school specialising in retail. The reasons that had led him there were becoming increasingly irrelevant. He had wanted to secure a job which was sufficiently well-paid to provide him with a decent lifestyle, but the syllabus and subjects studied and the approach to social issues (or the lack of it) had convinced him that it was not for him. So he was looking elsewhere.

We quickly agreed on a six-month internship at Pocheco, so we could work together and get to know each other. Then we made the link between our planned Eco*lo*nomy Centre and Tao, who took charge of this community project.

Then there is Louise, who successfully set up our reforestation project. It is plain to see that there are young professionals in our region, who with their wealth of conviction and experience, and passion for what they do, are not at all motivated by money for money's sake.

So young, but their ideas are already clear. As a company manager, I find that quite simply wonderful, a real inspiration. They demonstrate how to take things in hand without being overly nervous. Their people skills are so spontaneous that no obstacle stands in their way for long.

It all sounds as if I was born yesterday. But hearing never-ending complaints about the standstill in our 'education system gone awry', I had been swept along by the despondency of my generation which, like its predecessors, seems determined to be disappointed in the next generation.

Working differently

Tao, Louise and many other talented people working with us have demonstrated the enormous creativity of their ideas. I know from experience that if we company managers open the doors and windows and leave aside prejudice and convention (in recruitment, for instance), then great potential comes our way.

I wonder about this system that finds 'efficiency' in favouring cadres of engineers, technicians, salespeople, senior managers and lawyers, who all come out of the same schools, more or less, then go on to co-opt one another into public, semi-public or private companies. Their career path is practically set in stone by the time they are twenty-five. I find that quite sad.

I note that if four characteristics – integrity, intelligence, energy and reciprocity (which could also be called an ability for empathy, knowledge-sharing and responsibility) – are brought together, then diversity of professional backgrounds is as fertile for the worker as it is for the company and its business.

I fully agree that discipline and tenacity are necessary in business. But these qualities are also present in people who are self-taught... literary people whose training, believe me, demands no less discipline than training to be an engineer or a doctor. I can see (or imagine) that you are smiling, but try reading the works of our best classical and contemporary writers and philosophers... then we will come back to the subject of discipline and development of the mind!

Of course, we also pay attention to gender mix and parity and to getting a good mix of social, cultural and educational backgrounds. I'm not convinced that the best businesspeople are necessarily engineers or men.

It's mainly a question of training the mind to reason, which calls for widely varying and certainly less limited experience than the standard system offers. This is clear even in our little company.

There is no need to use the usual recruitment and psychometric tests that some schools train their students to take ("Hello! What do you like to do and what are you able to do? What would you like to be able to do that you are not able to do? What are your weak points, according to your friends?"). Nothing equals a direct, sincere, relaxed interview where people act naturally, without pretence or cheating.

From the manager's point of view, I think that this opportunity for stating the rules of the game with clarity should be seized upon. In our case, I base the relationship on a few simple principles. I explain, as precisely as possible, what we're looking for (although sometimes, the meeting unexpectedly inspires us to try something completely new). I also emphasise that we can only work well together if the relationship is based on reciprocity. We show trust spontaneously because we base our approach on relational integrity, intelligent dialogue and raw energy (these are actually the values described by the former chairman of a large corporation... so nobody is ever completely wrong!)

Why not be fair?

If we see eye to eye, we very quickly find a way of working together. It may take the form of an internship, and all work deserves its just rewards; there is no question of paying less than the minimum wage, even to interns, here at Pocheco. We are no richer than other companies, but we do consider that there is such a thing as a false economy.

Why pay trainees only two thirds of the minimum wage? Are they only required to supply two thirds of their energy, intelligence or integrity? Will they give any less of their time, effort or motivation than others, merely because they are learning? Are we not all constantly learning? Is there a workers' caste system, complete with untouchables?

Enough of this exploitation and penny-pinching, enough of this miserly and, basically, unproductive vision of the world of work! Admittedly work is expensive, but it is also profitable, as everyone knows.

Let projects mature

Moving outside one's comfort zone turns the company into a breeding ground of activity. I remember a session with the marketing team of a textile company. For several hours, we had been arguing about the clarity of our packaging and the consistency of our range, when I impulsively climbed onto the table. I was just messing around in an attempt to relax the atmosphere and liven my colleagues up, but I realised that I could suddenly see things from a different angle. It works very well, give it a try! One day, if someone catches you standing on your desk, you can blame me! Behaving in an unconventional way shouldn't obscure the fact that all acts and decisions demand the greatest discipline and attention. There is no contradiction in this. Of course we work hard, but a lot of it takes place unobserved – on the way back from a jog in the snowy countryside, when we finish a book, when we are watching a television programme (I believe in the virtues of boredom, in small doses of course!) or looking at an exhibition.

You have to give yourself a change of scene. From this point of view, questions of sustainable development present a vast array of new possibilities. Yvon Chouinard, who founded Patagonia, invented MBA or Management By Absence![2] He takes time to go round the world, and especially to climb all sorts of mountains, whenever possible. And his business is booming. He clears his head... as do his colleagues. I'm not talking about a round of golf once a week, but of giving others a breather. Giving them time to think about the business. Obviously, this also requires a clear structure and framework.

Mountaineering is not for me, heights make me dizzy! So I clear my head by going to see modern art (not by car or plane, but by train) and by reading. I go somewhere and write. Basically, I am not always hassling my colleagues. Everyone has breathing space. And the business comes to life, matures and sometimes takes on a very different character to anything I might have imagined. Sharing power and knowledge results in this kind of satisfaction, because we are not all-powerful and do not control everything all the time. This has nothing to do with neglect: clear rules have to be established. While reading a book by Jack Welch, the former chairman of General Electric,[3] I came across his formula for selecting colleagues – they should be intelligent, energetic and honest. Honest so that they do not use their energy and intelligence against the company's interests. With experience, I have added: reciprocity. In other words, conscious awareness of the existence of others, and that if they put a lot into the company, then their manager should reciprocate.

Reciprocity is another way of saying generosity, the idea of sharing and equitable collaboration. These are words which are a little old-fashioned. But I can live with that because of the satisfaction I feel from working with people who share such values.

Looking elsewhere for inspiration

To keep the company moving forward, never hesitate to look elsewhere for inspiration. For instance, anyone who knows the *Cartoucherie de*

---

2. In *Homme d'affaires malgré moi* (Businessman in spite of myself), Éditions Vuibert, 2007.

3. *Mes conseils pour réussir* (My advice for success), Jack Welch with Suzy Welch, Village Mondial, 2005.

Vincennes and its *Théâtre du Soleil*, presented by Ariane Mnouchkine, will understand where the inspiration for the development of Pocheco's Agora came from.

I still remember with great pleasure the shows and Shakespeare plays my parents took me to see in this wonderful place. Before the bell sounded, we would meet the actors while they were putting on their make-up and preparing for their roles, whilst we gazed, fascinated. Fascinated at witnessing this intimate moment, when each actor was transformed into their character. There were lights and mirrors, a sea of powder and make-up boxes, a messy whirl of heavy costumes, perfumes and tales that the actors would shortly be telling. It was like peeking at Shakespeare and Molière.

It was winter and the darkness only added to our wonder when the warm dressing room lights came into view in the distance. There was an exotic atmosphere conjured up by all this magic.

It was a place to encounter art, whether you were a theatre-lover or not. It seemed as if everyone had shed their everyday clothes and the burdens of daily life. At any rate, we came closer to art there than in the civilised and stuffy atmosphere of conventional theatres. The troupe's spirit seemed to emanate from the place, as if it had been chosen for this very reason.

Another example of finding inspiration in unlikely places: I sometimes take an hour out to go and visit a Norauto car repair workshop, with any lame excuse, just to see things from a different angle. I never cease to be amazed at their tidiness, organisation and their white gloves! At other times, I am full of admiration when I see hotel staff being briefed before they start their shift. And what could be more absorbing than a well-run building site? They should provide rows of seats so that spectators can applaud the graceful movements of joiners and masons.

You yourself have surely been hypnotised by a polishing machine gently gliding over the smooth floors of a railway station. And what about the extraordinarily precise ballet of trains arriving and departing?

There are many examples of systems working like these and it's often helpful to try to transpose such organisation or methods to our own workplace. I often annoy my colleagues with such ideas. It isn't always possible to transfer the techniques I observe, but the mere fact of wondering about it almost always gives rise to a new idea.

This is how things move forward on our production line and in our design office. For example, we rearrange our machines in the workshop, we question storage methods and the way people and things move around the factory. It keeps us watchful, and fit! We embrace change because routine bores us and may very well make us lose sight of customer satisfaction.

Nothing is more important than a relaxed, spontaneous discussion about an idea for production line lay-out or for the introduction of new technology. The workshop is under constant modification (as are the offices). One idea leads to another and the 'to do' list is added to on a regular basis. We reduced our energy consumption by two thirds, a process beginning with modifications to a noisy vacuum pump which was giving off a lot of unused heat, until we fitted it with heat recovery ventilators. We then decided to replace it with a newer-generation, more economical model, more flexible and better insulated, enabling us to recycle the excess energy for heating in the workshop. This improved working conditions, reduced risk and increased overall productivity.

An outside perspective and imagination

I strongly believe in the virtues of an outside perspective for turning the company into a pool of activity. I take part in meetings with technicians and listen to them explaining the difficulties of their work. I often get ideas in these cases. Being a non-specialist from outside their profession, I am always nervous that my ideas will sound absurd. However, I have never regretted expressing my views, which at worst are unsuitable and immediately forgotten. Often, though, my ideas have acted as a springboard for specialists to solve the problem in hand.

This is also why I favour a mix and diversity of origins and cultures in our teams. The variety of experience is interesting and we gain a great deal of intelligence and complementary knowledge. But, more than that, something very precious can arise from the effort each person makes to adapt to another's expertise and ideas.

This year, I began my meetings with the team leaders by asking them to close their eyes and think of Maria Callas. Then I suggested that they *were* Maria Callas, on stage at La Scala in Milan. I suggested that they could feel and imagine anything at all. Transporting ourselves by the power of imagination costs nothing. I base my way of working on this: the limitless ability to think and imagine. It opens new horizons.

But it's not all play. We are focused and hard-working, but we do not believe in taking ourselves too seriously in order to do a good job. I don't know who used this commonplace first. Many problems can be solved just by the distance humour offers. A little distance between us and events is often sorely lacking. People often neglect the essential and, as a result, cannot see the wood for the trees.

A great deal comes from a little imagination. I am not suggesting we put an end to planning, discipline and systematic checks. But I *am* suggesting a little eccentricity in addition to these three indispensable qualities. The sort of eccentricity that sometimes only comes to the surface among friends.

All too often, people veil their imagination, not wanting to show themselves up. Kings used to have jesters who, through humour or insolence, provided a useful step back from the problems in hand. Humour in the company need not be cynical or hurtful. It can quite simply be joyful, zany and funny. Imagination serves to defuse tension and pacify a situation.

Wherever I have worked, I have always been lucky enough to meet and spend time with real characters, big mouths with complex and engaging personalities. They have taught me a lot, although sometimes it was no joyride. But there have been a lot of laughs and the memories that stay with me are good. Real idiots are rarely funny, so I conclude that funny people are often intelligent.

A certain freedom

I have sometimes heard colleagues react with annoyance, "How dare you? You have no right to say that!" Such irritation, although quite common, is invariably counterproductive and always betrays a serious problem, with the person and/or the way the company functions. Flaubert had his shouting room, a place where he used to read his texts aloud so as to hear the sonority of his prose. His was the fundamental need of many creators: to speak their thoughts aloud in order to reformulate them and thus perfect them. Thoughts deserve to be expressed, pondered and worked on.

Success comes more easily if ideas and thoughts are expressed. Any system which closes in on itself collapses in the end. This being so, it only takes a second to understand that freedom of speech is vital, and I support it resolutely.

I have felt all too often that my proposals for change have been alarming. They have aroused hostility – I have even been made redundant because of them. Maybe I lacked diplomacy. I certainly underestimated the fact that in many traditional companies, presenting an idea is a privilege reserved exclusively for the boss. I have often observed bosses claiming ownership of ideas that were actually the brainchild of their colleagues.

Obstacles pile up at an alarming rate and feed on a hundred-and-one examples of cowardice or denial each day. Many people, when faced with making a decision, speak of the impossibility of change, because of 'company policy', or 'my line manager', or even better 'the management', or a refusal 'from above'. What a shame that certain workers only give themselves permission to say no! Even more often, I have watched their bosses let them get away with it.

I often say that my colleagues and I do not leave our brains in our lockers when we come to work (indeed, I have already said it in this book). The difficulties we overcome in our home lives provide us with opportunities for problem-solving. At work, we are faced with other sorts of problems, which we also overcome. Of course, expertise and in-house training help us to solve them, as long as we are not under stress or trying to offload our problems onto someone else. But I notice that a little responsibility at work does not make people any more stressed or ill, if the system permits movement, mistakes, sharing and thought. And if the environment is not so competitive that others are quick to take advantage of our mistakes.

Such are ideas... Good or bad, they are only thoughts, and as long as they remain so, they are to be welcomed. In contrast, stifling freedom of speech and expression of thoughts leads to stagnation. I believe we must always fight against the dangers of stagnation.

Chapter 12

Multiplying initiatives, even not for profit ones

A source of pride in our company is our ability to welcome projects which, at first sight, do not seem to have much to do with our main activity, but which provide the bond of a mutually-efficient collaboration between the world of work and the outside world.

I am impressed by the wealth of talent, ideas and expertise I meet. And I have realised that we have a real opportunity if we agree to listen, without negative bias, to those who approach us. The different forms of skills-based sponsorship make it possible, without spending much money, to devote a part of the workers' time to community activities, for example.[1] This is accessible to small firms like ours.

Bees on the roof

Like us, you will have heard that bees are dying of a strange condition[2] and that swarms which live on town roofs are surviving... because there are fewer pesticides in town air than in the fields! You will also know that if bees disappeared from the face of the Earth, humanity would quickly follow them, because pollination is absolutely vital for plants. Luckily, more and more beekeepers are finding solutions. One local beekeeper keeps hives on our planted roof. He comes regularly to look after them, and on each visit, a few of my colleagues accompany him and learn how to look after the bees themselves. What a pleasure it is, after all this work (do you know, for instance, that a bee visits 1,500

---

1. The Admical structure, presided over by Olivier Tcherniak and run by Bénédicte Menenteau and their team, will give you information and help. Go to www.admical.org

2. On this subject, I urge you to read *L'Étrange Silence des abeilles (The Strange Silence of Bees)*, Vincent Tardieu, Éditions Belin, 2009.

flowers just to collect one gramme of nectar?), to give out 300 kilogrammes of 'ecovelope honey' a year!

Since the cohabitation between humans and bees has caused no problems, we plan to increase the number of hives on our roofs.

Artists in residence

Even further from our main activity, we wanted to offer room for an artist in residence on our site. The idea came from a conversation I had in Berlin with an artist, who explained contemporary art to me and told me about the success of certain colleagues of his. They proceed like orchestra conductors: an idea and its concept give rise to developments that they supervise but do not carry out themselves. Why not welcome one at Pocheco? Their working methods might inspire us.

Since the successful launch of our reforestation organisation, the idea arose that our factory could house other activities, in addition to envelope manufacturing. Our open site could act as a pool for talents and ideas as well as for profit-based or non-profit enterprise (on condition that each activity is self-financing). It could even welcome artists in residence by offering them a studio to work in.

A CSA on site

In order to develop these community actions independently, we needed a place that would provide a link between our industrial activity and the village, where each could respect the other. Our Ecolonomy Centre (perhaps a world first!) arose from this idea. One way into our factory was along a cul-de-sac. A bakery had long stood at the end of this road, on a crossroads in the centre of the village. No one wanted to take the bakery over, so we bought it. This will become the missing link between us and the outside world.

It will house several community projects linked to the local, sustainable and durable economy. We are going to set up a CSA[3] project so that the villagers, as well as workers from Pocheco, can go once a week to buy a basket of fruit and vegetables grown by two farmers from the next village. The centre will also accommodate the

---

3. CSA: Community-supported agriculture, an association for the preservation of local farming.

headquarters of our reforestation organisation. There will even be a running club, bringing together amateurs and trainers. We will set up a café, for discussion and sharing information about new building techniques and the use of energy, materials and expertise. It will be a place for real, first-hand reflection on new ways of living and working.

I even hope that we will be able to lay the groundwork for other community partnerships, like the one I am already considering with the Baraka programme in Roubaix, whose aim is to involve locals in progressive social relations.

Louise and reforestation

When I met Louise, she was finishing a university course in environmental studies. She was having no luck in France finding a job with an environmental organisation. We were unable to find the time we needed to set up our reforestation organisation. Our region is a large plain of extremely fertile soil, rich in sand and clay. It is now very 'under-forested' and has been intensively exploited by agro-industry.

The Pocheco team set up logistic support and the company financed the first year of an organisation which Louise registered, enabling the first local reforestation groups to take action.

The first general meeting took place, with around thirty members, in late December 2009. The partnership came a long way in its first year, from its creation to the first 1,500 trees planted. It is highly encouraging to see how much local citizens want to act to help the environment and that it is possible, desirable even, to bring together citizens and local councils (which possess fallow land in our 'rurban' areas) with farmers. As surprising as it may seem, farmers, despite their initial mistrust, now support our action in ever-increasing numbers. The use of pesticides can be cut significantly simply by planting mixed hedgerows on the banks of ditches around a field – an 'ecolonomy' which helps re-establish biological diversity and reduces the risk of poisoning for farmers (of whom more and more are contracting cancer) and for consumers. Could there be any more satisfying result than watching the return to the ecosystem of ladybirds, frogs, small rodents, hedgehogs and the very shy, but useful, little owl? Replanting protective areas develops biological corridors where animal species can once again reproduce in safety.

There are multiple benefits, including social interaction. Private companies and other types of organisation can work together!

A scrumping orchard

In partnership with the farmers and council of Forest-sur-Marque, we have already rehabilitated fallow land and areas which have been used for illegal flytipping. We have also planted around 500 trees and shrubs, on Alan's initiative (Alan has been managing our reforestation association since Louise left to further her education at the University of Vancouver), to create an orchard for the village children to discover the pleasure of picking naturally-grown apples with different flavours. We would like rare varieties to be preserved and contribute to the mission of the regional nature conservation agency.

Our conservation orchard may well become a nursery. We have involved agricultural colleges, whose students help to plant and look after rare species.

As well as an orchard, we are also replanting shrubs around the edge of cultivated land to protect biodiversity. The farmer was able to cut his use of pesticides by three-quarters last year. Not only did he make a substantial financial saving, but he was also able to reduce the health risk to himself and to the people who buy his cereals. The introduction of 'insect hotels' has the added value of bringing back bumblebees, butterflies and, at the water's edge, dragonflies. It has even witnessed the invention and scattering of 'seed grenades'. The 'seed grenade', Alan's brainchild, is made of seeds from a variety of plants compacted into a little dried compost and wrapped in small biodegradable-paper sachets. The seeds germinate in the rain and the wind spreads the plants and flowers to re-establish some badly-needed biodiversity.

A question of advertising?

The question of decompartmentalisation must be raised in the context of the collaboration between the company and the community.

At the first general meeting of Pocheco Canopée Reforestation, members questioned me on the link I wished to make between the non-profit organisation and the private company that I manage. The basic question was: "Why have you kept the company's name in the title of the reforestation organisation, if not for free publicity?"

Doing Business and Manufacturing Differently

I started by reminding them that without the Pocheco team, their project would never have seen the light of day. Pocheco is a private company which would be nothing but an empty, useless shell were it not run by and for its employees. The employees and their boss are not capitalists motivated only by greed. The team remain active citizens even at work. Like everybody, they are concerned by the social challenges facing us all. And, like all citizens, they want to find ways of taking action. The company is a springboard.

Furthermore, the company has long-established relationships with banks, customers, local citizens and service providers. It has enabled the development of social interaction. If we develop projects, they are more solid because they are built on the already-existing foundation of the company.

Finally, our creations are not necessarily productive from a financial point of view. Economic profitability is not the only aim of society. Why build impenetrable walls between the different forms of human activity?

We must not mix everything up. Our laws are extremely clear. All we have to do is apply them. There's no law against forming a partnership like this.

"Are you doing it for publicity?"

No.

Our name is unknown to the general public. And we would have nothing to gain by being better known. Our clients entrust their production to us because we are competitive and reliable, not because we are well-known! Their purchasing departments will not come to us because we have set up this reforestation organisation or because we are environmental activists.

Yes, our company bears a name which represents a company initiative devised and supported by a team. It backs an economic scheme and a community project. The project of a tightly-knit, open and active team.

Partnerships between volunteers, paid staff and private companies can act together – aware, responsible and working together, rather than all against one another. What is there to stop them?

Why do we never think to question what commercial television and radio relentlessly thrust before us, yet are so quick to distrust charities, non-profit organisations and companies that try to work together?

If we become excessively divided and individualistic, we will not be able to think and work together. We must not forget that there is strength in numbers, and this is one of the solutions for collectively bringing about the conditions for the economic upturn.

PART FOUR

A New Company Model

"From dream to reality?"

Ec*olo*nomy is making great strides. To illustrate this, I have chosen to present two eco*lo*nomical experiments carried out by companies of varying size and activity.

Case Study:

Guy Watson, founder of Riverford Organic Farms

Riverford Farm grows vegetables for organic veg boxes and Guy Watson, is a charismatic, 'left-leaning' Devon farmer with a mission: to provide fresh, flavoursome and local produce (sold in vegetable boxes) for the families in his region and further afield. When the scheme started, he was selling thirty boxes a week to his friends and family. Today he sends 47,000 boxes all over the country thanks to the partnerships he has cultivated with other farmers. He used to sell to supermarkets and detested the money-based, unilateral negotiations which took place between him and a buyer who "knows no more about vegetables than the biscuits he was trading last week".[1] His passion for his vegetables is evident. His farm is organic, not only because he is passionately committed to reducing its impact on the environment but also because he believes that the taste and flavour of his vegetables is far superior to anything found on the shelves of the supermarket. He recounts a trip to visit a conventional farmer on the Fens:

He was growing lettuces for the supermarket and I bent down to pick a bit of Escarolles and he said "I shouldn't do that, boy! Because it's been sprayed, it's sprayed every week for aphids". And I thought, hang on, this is a farmer who won't eat his own food. Intuitively, anybody knows that's crazy! Food should be fit to be eaten straight out of the field.

And so his farms are managed organically, with no pesticides or fertilisers. He combats pests naturally, spraying aphids with soap or releasing natural predators such as ladybirds and parasitic wasps to protect his crops: he even voluntarily deploys pests onto his crops to encourage predators and to trigger the natural cycle of defence. He is considering transforming some of his greenhouses into a biosphere in which pests and predators can grow in symbiosis until their springtime

---

1. *The Daily Telegraph* 29/05/15.

release into the fields. Fertilisers are replaced with manure and natural compost and the farmer plants Alexander clover in August which is then mown down in November. The plant leaves natural residues of nitrogen as well as aerating the soil and prepares the ground naturally for the next crops.

There is no replacement for small-scale mixed farming, relying on natural predators, hedgerows, flowering plants and trees to ensure a sustainable source of delicious vegetables.

And it makes his farm a pleasant place to work and to live.

It is easy to forget how beautiful Devon is, especially at the start of summer with the crops looking full of vigour.[2]

And yet his preoccupation with nature is not limited to his immediate environment. He agrees with Pocheco that a long-term model is more sustainable and that production techniques which respect the wider environment are more economically interesting.

All of the profits from the farm are reinvested back into the business: apart from the end of year bonuses which are redistributed between the 500 members of the team. Guy is vociferous when it comes to making his business fit the current mindset. His is not a flexible model. He is subject to the vagaries of the weather and of the rhythm of his crops, hardly compatible with the way of thinking of the free market, which lauds flexibility, responsiveness and immediacy. Far from exploiting natural resources, he must respect and protect them if he wishes his business to thrive.

A two year collaborative project with The University of Exeter and the Department of Trade and Industry under the 'Knowledge Transfer Partnership' programme allowed him to work with the university to study the environmental impacts of his farm and activity. They carried out a study of their carbon footprint in which they discovered that after transport, the most CO_2-heavy part of the business was the packaging used for the veg boxes.

Packaging makes up a staggering 17% of our carbon footprint, and this only accounts for manufacturing the materials as this is the best data we can get at the moment. From the start, we have worked hard to come up

---

2. *The Daily Telegraph* 29/05/15.

> with what we thought were environmentally-sensible solutions to packaging, so we were surprised to find that this formed such a large part of our carbon footprint. Our research has led us to believe that some of our efforts and much of the publicity around less damaging packaging is mis-guided and actually obstructing real progress. Despite the green proclamations of many of our supermarkets, to date they have excluded packaging from their carbon footprints. Though this is perfectly acceptable under common carbon accounting methodologies I would certainly argue that they are morally responsible for this packaging, especially as it is supermarkets that have largely driven the move towards ever higher and more absurd levels of packaging.[3]

Riverford respected the 'Reduce, Reuse, Recycle' maxim and started by redesigning their packaging to reduce weight and thickness. Their customers are already pretty aware and accept cauliflower, cabbage and lettuce with only their natural protection – the thick outer leaves. The packaging extras, such as netting for the onions and plastic bagging for the carrots seems to further distance the customer from the natural state of the products and he is constantly on the look out for ways to reduce these extraneous layers.

The farm looked into replacing its plastic bags with biodegradable plastic bags.

> *Theoretically the bags are great because they break down in sunlight or air. But they cannot be recycled, and they cannot be composted, so inevitably end up in landfill, generating greenhouse gases as they break down. We started using them with the best intentions but it was a bad decision, based on biased information from manufacturers.*

The counterintuitive nature of this experience is one reason why it is so important to acquire objective, scientific data rather than trusting the evidence of our senses. Another example is the transport of our food. We tend to believe that it makes more ecological sense to consume food produced locally, which in an ideal world, it does. But his customers, forward thinking as they are, want variety and sometimes more exotic produce in their veg boxes. Although 80% of the produce he sells is home-grown, he is obliged to reconcile the

---

3. This and subsequent quotes are taken from the company's website: www.riverford.co.uk

demands of his customers with his own desire to protect his environment.

'Local' is commonly assumed to be best for the environment, but when it comes to heated glasshouse crops this is often not the case. Even with the help of tunnels or glass, without heating, tomatoes can only be harvested in this country from July to October. The bulk of the crop is harvested in August and September; a very short season even for the most die-hard seasonal eater. Intensive, highly professional hot house producers plant their crops in heated greenhouses in January or February so they can harvest from March or April through to November or December. This produces prolific yields over a long season but only at the expense of huge amounts of heat which is normally produced by burning gas or oil. For every kilo of tomatoes picked, two to three kg of CO_2 are released into the atmosphere. By comparison it is possible to produce tomatoes in the south of Spain or Italy, without heat, right through the winter (though heat is still sometimes used to improve the quality and consistency of the crop). The emissions from transporting those tomatoes to the UK (about 240g of CO_2 per kg of fruit) are about a tenth of those associated with growing them closer to home using heat.

The impact of importing food from abroad is often measured in so-called 'food miles'. However this indicator doesn't take into account the volume of food carried by a vehicle or the variation in greenhouse emissions of different forms of transport (the most emission-heavy part of a product's transport is often the shortish car journey from supermarket to home) or the electricity needed to heat greenhouses. And so he has no problem selling tomatoes cultivated in Spain or peppers from Morocco because he analyses the impact of these purchases and then works to decrease it: no air freight, ship rather than road where possible, full lorries when road transport is necessary. And he is on a mission to educate his customers and change their purchasing habits and expectations: he writes a weekly newsletter and his website is full of impassioned articles. He also writes in several national newspapers.

Common sense solutions implemented on the farm allow him to save money and reduce his environmental impact. The cold stores used to preserve his produce once picked consume significant amounts of electricity: 70% of his total usage. But dusting the heat exchangers, insulating, shutting doors and raising awareness has allowed the farm to reduce its consumption. The excess heat from the cold stores is used to dry onions and also to heat the buildings. He no longer pays for any heating. His next project is to generate electricity through a system of anaerobic digestion. Organic matter is left to ferment in oxygen-free conditions, thereby releasing methane which can then be used as fuel. He wants to get together with local businesses to collect their waste matter too. And his long term plan is to install a wind turbine, although he predicts planning permission problems.

His staff of 500 are content. The salary differential is 1:8. They know they will not make a fortune but are happy to work for the 'good guys'. He wants to involve them even more closely in the decision-making process and envisages making the company into a *"mutual, to be owned by staff and customers"*. More than just a farm, Riverford has become a laboratory for testing new techniques, reducing environmental impact and putting flavour before profit and scientific proof before marketing advantage.

Interview:

Éric Sauvage, Co-founder and manager of TexEurop

Emmanuel DRUON: I'd like to hear your account of TexEurop. Why you decided on this profession twenty years ago, what the original idea was and how you have built up a company which now works on several continents and manufactures 25 million items per year.

Éric SAUVAGE: I came into the textile industry by chance. TexEurop was founded in 1991. At the start, we worked in part in France, where we dyed our products, especially with dyers in the Nantes area. We did pongee dying, in response to increasing demand from customers. Fashion was working on ever-shorter cycles, production costs were rising in Europe and the textile industry here was losing out to countries with low labour costs, particularly China. Customs tariffs dropped significantly, making large-scale imports, especially from Eastern Europe, more and more competitive. Our customers left us… in search of products with ever-lower production costs. To keep our customers, we had to follow and begin working with the Far East and Eastern Europe. We began working in Poland in 1992. I saw the Russians leave Warsaw when the Berlin Wall came down. We started with Poland, and from there we went immediately to Romania and Lithuania. We stayed ten years in Romania. We applied the Benetton model, so to speak: our weaving was done in Poland and Romania and our pongee articles, our unbleached products, were dyed in France. We responded to customer requests job by job. On Monday morning, there would be a phone call: "Have you got something cheap in baby pink?" and we would have to come up with it in three days.

Working in France was very expensive. More and more retail purchasers were thinking along purely administrative lines, without any regard for the product itself. We were forced to stop our pongee production in France, Belgium and Italy and make the finished product in Eastern Europe, then in Asia.

From the moment when Europe decreased its customs tariffs and many Asian countries abolished quotas, we were inundated with low-cost products and anyone wishing to carry on working with retail had to follow suit.

ED: And what about agriculture?

ÉS: I studied horticulture and arboriculture and went in for the transformation of wood. I personally own a forestry company, with forests mainly in France, in the Haute-Loire, and now also in the Cher, near Bourges. We grow sessile oak for timber – it's used for storing vintage wines in Bordeaux. Then we have more resinous woods, used for building: spruce, fir, beech and larch. It's a job I love, it's something very personal, it enables me to recover my own ecological fibre and to transform wood with respect for the natural cycle of the trees and forest. The forest has to be maintained, it's an extremely long-term investment. You don't invest in a forest as you would in a normal product, given that a tree lives for a minimum of 40 or 50 years. When you manage the forest with respect, you come back to your own values. It's a satisfying investment for a sensitive person. There's a spiritual dimension to being in the forest, it's magnificent. The earth is not any old product. When you work the land, you have to listen to it and respect it. Today, when you are in the forest, you must honour the land to be in tune with its values and respect the plants' natural cycle, much as farmers do. It gives me enormous satisfaction and pleasure.

ED: So, you manage a great company with a very high turnover at the same time as developing another business, which is closer to your convictions?

ÉS: Yes, it's a pleasure and a joy. When you work, you need to stick to your principles and surround yourself with very good people. The forest is special, because you don't have to go there every day. There are good times of the year to fell trees. As long as you're there when it's necessary, there's no trouble. I don't manage the forest personally, I have a team, it's a question of organisation. It's different to a company that you have to manage day in, day out, where there's still a notion of pleasure, but which needs more complex management. When you exploit (or work, to use a less pejorative word) the forest, you have to take the regulations into account and respect nature. We're in a world where no one respects anyone else and where they respect nature even less. We are the only living species which does not respect its environment. We are destroying everything. If we don't live in harmony with our natural habitat, I don't see how we're going to manage.

ED: How can you reconcile this difficulty, this contradiction, when you are a manufacturer and your product has a very short life cycle? Some of your customers must listen with great attention when you speak about your environmental, ecological and human convictions. Do they allow for this when it comes to price? Are they prepared to pay extra? Do they get the message?

ÉS: It isn't always easy. Some customers accept it, others listen, and others don't pay attention because they have tight margins. In general, it's the consumer who decides. We've been battling for years for organic cotton, we want it to be used in preference to traditional cotton, even though we have no direct contact with the consumer.

ED: Tell me about organic cotton.

ÉS: Conventional cotton is really destructive for the planet. It's farmed intensively and dries up the water table, as well as using a lot of pesticides. 1 kilo of cotton consumes 10,000 litres of water! 30% of all pesticides sold are used in cotton farming. Once you've farmed cotton, you can plant nothing else. The plant is heavy on water and dries the ground out. In India, water tables have dropped by 150 metres in 20 or 30 years, not to mention being polluted by pesticides. The consequences are direct for health and indirect for ecology. So we have tried to use organic cotton as much as we can, even though there's a slight difference in price, but it's not always easy because our customers always demand margins.

ED: How is organic cotton better?

ÉS: It's farmed in a way which respects the land and doesn't dry it out and no pesticides are used. It's similar to what we do in Europe with organic food crops. Many factors come into play. Care is taken with the environment, the soil and health. It's like going back to the agriculture of the old days: before feeding the plant, they feed the soil. This means cutting out mineral fertilisers and replacing them with organic fertilisers. Today, however, people only feed the plant without respecting the earth, which leads to the impoverishment of the soil and creates deserts in the wake of intensive farming.

ED: It's very interesting that you say organic cotton is only slightly more expensive.

ÉS: Organic cotton is generally between 10 and 15% more expensive, depending on quality. To give you a price, let's imagine that I sell a good-quality tee-shirt for €3 - with organic cotton it would cost €3.10-€3.20.

ED: A difference which guarantees that the earth is worked with respect for natural cycles. This implies pumping much less from the water table and in a different way.

ÉS: That happens if crops are correctly rotated. If farming is very intensive, as it was in Uzbekistan, where the Aral Sea disappeared, the earth dies completely because cotton exhausts it. The same plant needs the same elements all the time. If you grow another plant afterwards, it takes different elements from the soil. Certain plants need a lot of nitrogen, others need dietary minerals, etc. Each plant has different natural needs. By rotating crops, you aren't always draining the soil of the same things. Enriching the soil, as farmers used to do, improves its structure, which in turn helps the plants. The plant becomes more resistant and requires fewer products, notably pesticides, to keep it healthy. If you respect the plant's natural cycle, it develops natural resilience. I know this from experience - my forests in the Haute-Loire also resist fierce storms. There's never one single species in a forest, you see silver birches, oaks, spruces, ashes, etc.

Nature is common sense. Man has done everything topsy-turvy so as to increase productivity and, in the process, has torn everything apart. We're paying the price of intensive farming today. It's all a question of common sense.

ED: Can you find the organic cotton that you need?

ÉS: We can find some. It's difficult because you need to know the right people, but we can find it. On the other hand, our customers don't always want to pay for it. We are not in a position to impose it on them, but when they want organic cotton, we can supply them with all the correct certifications, we've carried out audits, everything's crystal-clear. What we need is for the consumer to get involved, but that remains a sticking point. Consumers are very receptive to organic food, but there's still a lot of work to do when it comes to organic clothing.

ED: So basically, the retailers' position will change if the consumer's attitude changes?

ÉS: Yes, consumers must be aware of this.

ED: Have there been comparative studies, along the lines of an LCA, between a tee-shirt in conventional cotton and a tee-shirt in organic cotton? Has your sector already worked on this?

ÉS: Yes, of course! Both our sector and the NGOs have studied it, it's very important. All the more so because conventional cotton, due to companies like Monsanto, has been genetically modified. It's serious. And because cotton is grown in countries where there's a great deal of corruption.

ED: You're an industrialist and transformer?

ÉS: First and foremost, we're industrialists. Our factory provides a living for 3,400 people in Bangladesh. And we employ 30,000 people through sub-contracting, with contracts certified by our customers. I've been working with Bangladesh for twenty years. When I first went, people said, "He's mad! What's he going to do over there? There's nothing there except water and cyclones!" I found the country and its people endearing. They are honest, it took me back to the authenticity there used to be among the country people in France years ago. We decided to do something good in Bangladesh. We didn't want to develop there like certain people, who exploit kids and take advantage of local poverty. We were the first to invest massively in Bangladesh, several million dollars. We set up factories with French teams in the country, we imported machinery, especially from Germany, Italy and Switzerland. We went about things exactly as we would have in Europe. We decided to follow the directives of the ILO (International Labour Organisation), namely no overtime, or at least paid overtime, 3 months' maternity leave for pregnant women, the first crèches in Bangladesh. Today, we are recognised for manufacturing in the best conditions, even if it's a country where labour costs are a fraction of those in other countries.

ED: Is that why you went there, or was it to get closer to the raw material?

ÉS: We went for both reasons – the raw materials come from southeast Asia (as well as Egypt and the United States) and labour costs there are low. But with transport costs constantly rising, we now prefer to produce where we sell. The future, in any case, lies in producing where we sell.

ED: The factory you developed in the 1990s must be unique.

ÉS: It is. We really did things properly. With Okaïdi, the chain store for children which has created foundations all over Morocco and Pakistan, we are setting up a foundation focusing on microcredit, with our surplus stock and seconds. We give training and teach a trade to homeless women who have nothing, and they produce articles. We then sell these articles on microcredit, for a few symbolic dakas.

The aim is for the women to sell their products to other women, who then sell them on stalls all over the country. It enables them to earn a bit of money and support themselves.

ED: So, the aim is to get women working?

ÉS: Yes. It's a Muslim country where women are excluded from economic life. Our objective is to bring women into the economic world so that they can be independent.

ED: A factory in Bangladesh, offices in Asia, soon a factory in Europe?

ÉS: We would like to buy a factory in Treviso for our European production. In the long run, with transport, energy and logistics costs rising continually, manufacturing in Asia will become less and less profitable.

ED: What kind of products will you make in the Treviso factory?

ÉS: Top-of-the-range products. We work with shops that want low prices, but we also have customers who are looking for quality. With shorter cycles and lower quantities, southern Europe is interesting for us nowadays. We would have two sites to work on other kinds of products: one in Portugal, in Porto, and the other in Italy. The minimum wage in Portugal is €470 euros, and our salaries in China (because we also have a factory near Shenzhen) are around €300 euros, which coupled with transport costs works out about the same.

ED: Yours is an activity based around the production of a raw material which, in its conventional form, poses a serious environmental problem. You are trying to solve the problem by orientating more and more international customers towards natural, organic products. What percentage of your orders does organic cloth account for at present?

ÉS: I'm ashamed to tell you, because it's not much. We have customers where it's 10 or 15%, but there aren't many of them. It's micro-action, everyone's doing their little bit. I try to follow my conscience. For instance, when I'm walking along the beach in Brittany and I find a plastic bottle, I pick it up. I pick up plastic bags in the forest. Sometimes it's a real pest, I come back with my arms full, but I can't stop myself doing it. That's how I am, I love nature and I do what I can on my level.

In a company, you have to use the least-polluting materials and carry out daily tasks with a certain logic... knowing that if you produce, you pollute. We try to have the lowest carbon footprint possible for our products in terms of logistics. For example, we try to bring our sites closer together and this is why we have chosen to manufacture in southern Europe. We will be able to produce closer to home and offer work to Europeans. This is important because unemployment leads to poverty, which can lead to a rise in extremist political movements. Unemployment will lead us into a dictatorship within thirty years...

ED: I would like to pick on what you said about micro-action: it's better to start small than to do nothing.

ÉS: I try to think of the kids in Bangladesh as my own children and have consideration for them. I respect their environment. Many manufacturers have relocated because environmental standards are very strict in Europe. They said that in Bangladesh or in India, you could bribe dodgy politicians and chuck everything in the rivers. We built a water-treatment plant up to European standards. But there are groups of Chinese or Americans, notably working for Walmart, whose only worry is the price. Too bad if the water table is polluted, as long as it's not where they come from. The planet is a village as far as I'm concerned. We mustn't do things in other places that we would not consider doing at home, it's a matter of conscience. I can no more throw litter on the ground in Bangladesh than I can in a French forest.

ED: It's also a question of proper behaviour! Building a water-treatment plant is an exceptional step, but it *should* be the norm! The same applies to acting in accordance with the highest existing standards, because people are the same everywhere, with the same rights and duties.

ÉS: We're living in a schizophrenic and cynical world. I always work on the principle that it's better to be right on your own than wrong all together. You have to make choices in line with your own conscience. I have competitors who don't do things the same way as me and who are cheaper. Of course they are, they have no water-treatment plant to run.

ED: Are they really cheaper?

ÉS: They are! But I prefer to lose sales than to go in that direction. I have lost customers, especially in this region, big customers that you know, because I couldn't respond to their demands on price. They don't give a hoot about the water-treatment plant. They say, "I want such-and-such a price, get on with it!"

ED: They have a very short-term view where you're constantly in competition and where only the price counts…

ÉS: They pretend to do this or that (greenwashing, in reality), but in fact, the person who offers a product 5% or 10% cheaper gets the contract. I try to remain philosophical, because it's difficult to change the world on your own. People do want to consume better; it started with food and it's going to happen with textiles, but it takes time. We're nearing the end of an economic system which is no longer viable. If we want to carry on consuming as we are, we will need eight planets like the Earth.

ED: Do you think that the acceleration of human folly will lead us more quickly into a complete reversal of the situation?

ÉS: Some people are becoming aware of the situation. Young people don't want to consume like we did, they're more careful. Things will change thanks to them, it's absolutely essential.

Conclusion

Ec*olo*nomy, the ambitious choice of the new economy

I do not believe for one second in the 'deindustrialisation' that we have been told is coming, but rather in the new impetus brought about by the innovation we find when we apply sustainable development practices to our business activities. Business in the 21st century can and must pay great attention and devote substantial resources to a re-industrialisation which meets new eco*lo*nomical standards. There is a lot to do, but it is possible.

Favouring the circular economy

This ambitious objective is to orientate our choices towards a circular economy: by reducing our impact on the environment with each investment; by producing the energy we need locally and by constantly making our production tools more competitive; by treating our dirty effluents on-site, rather than sending them over long distances, by way of complicated networks which are difficult to maintain.

Today, water agencies propose on-site treatment and choose to abandon the 20th-century concept of mains drainage. By sorting and treating as much as possible on-site, companies and local authorities reduce their ecological impact. And they develop new services and jobs.

Producing energy is becoming more and more possible for everyone. So is reducing energy consumption. To achieve this, time and means are absolutely essential: reducing the plague of 'short-termism' linked to immediate or very rapid financial profit; building a society better adapted to individual needs: a job, development of knowledge, sharing responsibilities according to one's professional development and training.

A growing number of small companies and the shareholders who lead them must also accept that development takes time and that companies can be passed on from generation to generation. Growth is worthless if it is built on sand.

Giving a dimension to growth

However, growth is possible at a reasonable pace. This means taking notice of the idea that a useful, well-made product lasts much longer; that the resource is renewable and that the end of a product's life is only envisaged in terms of recycling and re-use – once again: for our envelopes, the paper manufacturers fell 60,000 trees and plant 200,000 yearly, in complete respect for the biodiversity of species and spaces. In this way, they and our customers contribute to the expansion of European forest by 4.3% a year.

I sincerely believe that if human genius is capable of inventing the atom bomb, then it is surely capable of inventing the circular economy! If people believed, in the past, that gigantism was the solution and that they were able to invent hydroelectric dams or nuclear power stations, then any engineer nowadays must certainly be capable of inventing the tools of deconstruction. For instance, it is conceivable that the work of the nuclear power companies could be, for at least fifty years to come, the dismantling and remediation of nuclear sites.

Citizenship doesn't stop at the company's front door

Politicians and the elite are not the only ones able to bring about change. The will to change belongs to the people, they only need to exercise it! To this end, skills – wherever they may be found – should be brought together rather than split apart.

On the scale of our little industrial company, caught in the credit crunch and a collapsing market, we progress regularly and produce smoothly. We join-up talent. Each day, we edge a little closer to our projects becoming self-financing. Each year, we strengthen our equity and our colleagues' expertise. The whole team plays a part in Pocheco's move towards a circular economy and a system that will make our development progressive and gradual, sustainable – once and for all – from the point of view of our team, their environment and the natural resources of our unique planet.

California has become the eighth world power with its Silicon Valley. The Nord-Pas-de-Calais, an industrial region, which is reborn from its ashes once a century, can become Ecolonomy Valley. Our polluted soil, contaminated water tables, air laden with microparticles, ageing nuclear power station and our 14% unemployment rate are all challenges that can be turned to our advantage. We should give the means to our young people, who are talented and multi-ethnic but not sufficiently involved in the world of work, to energise our regional economy. Every day, we meet eco*lo*nomical apprentices who are not caught up in consumerism and who have decided to change the world and make it liveable again in the long term.

How? By understanding that not only is ecology not a rude word, but that it is the most economical solution that can be found. At Pocheco, we have been coming through economic downturns for twenty years by reducing our impact on the environment. It is more economical to work ecologically. Waste is a resource. We should depollute the land with plants, collect and recycle heavy metals, produce energy where it is needed, and bring trade and production back to the heart of our towns. Our international expansion will be carried out collectively by rolling out our expertise in countries where there is demand for these gentle techniques of producing energy and reprocessing waste. Like open source software, we are ready to share our knowledge and allow others to adapt it to their needs; the technology exists, all it takes is commitment. We are not in a crisis, we are in a transition and it is a wonderful opportunity for entrepreneurs. It is up to you! The whole Pocheco team and I would be very happy to welcome you, to discuss our proposals and actions in the common aim of finding, together, innovative and better-adapted solutions for companies and society. And, of course, for the environment.

Solutions exist, all we have to do is think about them together.

Notice

With my publisher, I chose a printer for this book with PEFC, FSC and SFI Chain of Custody (CoC) certification. CoC is an accounting system that tracks wood fibre through the different stages of production: from the forest, to the mill, to the paper, to the printer and ultimately to the finished book. CoC ensures the integrity of the paper supply chain and that the paper used is from responsibly managed forests. Professional forestry consists of phases of cutting and replanting. When planting programmes respect natural diversity, they preserve the soil and allow for the sustainable presence of fauna and flora. Planting trees at the same rate as we cut them down means that carbon dioxide, which causes the greenhouse effect, can be absorbed. Responsible forest management implies thinning out: space is left by cutting down certain trees and leaving others to grow taller and longer. The forest is correctly maintained, thereby reducing the risk of devastation by fire or disease. Using paper is, then, part of the struggle against global warming.

I thank my publishers for agreeing not to publish this book in electronic format. The impact of the ebook on the environment remains poorly understood and is extremely detrimental. The first LCAs available confirm that digital equipment, IT servers, personal computers (like the one I'm writing on now) and network systems, connection leads, underground (or underwater) cable networks, transmission masts and satellites, consume a great deal of energy in their production, for transport and for data sorting, as well as for cooling servers. Digital equipment consumes large quantities of petrochemicals and mined raw materials, including materials which are becoming ever-scarcer and cannot be replaced in the human time scale. Certain precious metals and solvents are harmful. Recycling of our electronic waste has not yet been mastered in a controlled and sustainable fashion.

From this point of view, paper, which consumes water, additives, transport and wood for its production, is a tried and tested material and its environmental impact is fully understood. Paper recycling has been mastered (even if much room for improvement persists, especially in the area of waste collection).

For all these reasons, I have chosen the conventional paper format, thereby remaining loyal to the ideas set out in this book.

Emmanuel Druon

Acknowledgements

My Colleague Elizabeth Dinsdale has been extremely diligent in reading, rereading, amending and reorganising the chapters of this book, and it is no exaggeration to write that, without her, I would never have managed it. Without the critical rereading of Réjean Dorval, Anne Berriat, Lionel and Quentin Hodara and research by Élodie Bia, Tao Carpentier and Kévin Franco, I would never have completed this little book. I thank them for their analyses and their ideas.

Contacting Pocheco

You can contact Pocheco:

In writing:

Pocheco
13, rue des Roloirs
59510 Forest-sur-Marque
France

Pocheco organises conferences and themed visits for groups (in French, English, German, Spanish and Greek) at the same address, by appointment. Élodie Bia or Elizabeth Dinsdale will be happy to provide you with further information.

By phone:
+33 320 61 90 90

By email:
ecolonomies@pocheco.com

Online at:
www.pocheco.com

About the Publisher

Triarchy Press is an independent publisher of new alternative thinking (altThink) about organisations and society – and practical ways to apply that thinking. Where Emmanuel Druon talks about dismantling our preconceived ideas and taking individual, organisational and collective responsibility for thinking and acting differently, he exemplifies what we see as the kind of practical hope and wise initiative inspired by altThink.

Other titles from Triarchy Press:

Restoring practical hope and inspiring wise initiative are two of the intentions of International Futures Forum – one of Triarchy's Publishing Partners. IFF's books on designing resilience, transformative innovation in education, Three Horizons thinking and things to do in a conceptual emergency have all been published by Triarchy Press.

Planning for the future is also a highly technical matter and one of the longest-established and most highly valued approaches is Scenario Planning. *Facing the Fold* brings together a collection of the best essays on the subject by one of its leading proponents, James (Jay) Ogilvy.

Stephen Millett's guide to forecasting and planning, *Managing the Future* offers a straightforward and pragmatic approach to strategic planning in business. Alongside it, Patricia Lustig's *Strategic Foresight* offers leaders a set of tools for navigating into an uncertain future.

Ecovillage brings together an inspiring selection of ecovillage community projects from all over the world while Daniel Wahl's *Regenerative Cultures* looks at the whole range of initiatives driving a revolution in agriculture, industry, trade, finance, community living and education around the world.

Details of all these titles can be found at:

www.triarchypress.net/the-future

Lightning Source UK Ltd.
Milton Keynes UK
UKOW06f1002031115

261979UK00008B/143/P

9 781909 470866